112TH CONGRESS 2nd Session	SENATE	REPORT 112–167

INQUIRY INTO COUNTERFEIT ELECTRONIC PARTS IN THE DEPARTMENT OF DEFENSE SUPPLY CHAIN

———

R E P O R T

———

of the

COMMITTEE ON ARMED SERVICES
UNITED STATES SENATE

MAY 21, 2012.—Ordered to be reported on May 21, 2012.

———

U.S. GOVERNMENT PRINTING OFFICE

WASHINGTON : 2012

COMMITTEE ON ARMED SERVICES

CARL LEVIN, Michigan, *Chairman*

JOSEPH I. LIEBERMAN, Connecticut
JACK REED, Rhode Island
DANIEL K. AKAKA, Hawaii
E. BENJAMIN NELSON, Nebraska
JIM WEBB, Virginia
CLAIRE McCASKILL, Missouri
MARK UDALL, Colorado
KAY R. HAGAN, North Carolina
MARK BEGICH, Alaska
JOE MANCHIN III, West Virginia
JEANNE SHAHEEN, New Hampshire
KIRSTEN E. GILLIBRAND, New York
RICHARD BLUMENTHAL, Connecticut

JOHN McCAIN, Arizona
JAMES M. INHOFE, Oklahoma
JEFF SESSIONS, Alabama
SAXBY CHAMBLISS, Georgia
ROGER F. WICKER, Mississippi
SCOTT P. BROWN, Massachusetts
ROB PORTMAN, Ohio
KELLY AYOTTE, New Hampshire
SUSAN M. COLLINS, Maine
LINDSEY GRAHAM, South Carolina
JOHN CORNYN, Texas
DAVID VITTER, Louisiana

RICHARD D. DeBobes, *Staff Director*
ANN E. SAUER, *Minority Staff Director*

————

INVESTIGATION TEAM

JOSEPH M. BRYAN, *Majority Professional Staff Member*
ILONA R. COHEN, *Majority Counsel*
OZGE GUZELSU, *Majority Counsel*

————

BRYAN D. PARKER, *Minority Investigative Counsel*

————

BRADLEY S. WATSON, *Staff Assistant*

TABLE OF CONTENTS

EXECUTIVE SUMMARY

"We do not want a $12 million missile defense interceptor's reliability compromised by a $2 counterfeit part."

> General Patrick O'Reilly
> Director, Missile Defense Agency
> November 8, 2011

The systems we rely on for national security and the protection of our military men and women depend on the performance and reliability of small, incredibly sophisticated electronic components. Our fighter pilots rely on night vision systems, enabled by transistors the size of paper clips, to identify targets. Our soldiers and Marines depend on radios and GPS devices, and the microelectronics that make them work, to stay in contact with their units and get advance warning of threats that may be around the next corner. The failure of a single electronic part can leave a soldier, sailor, airman, or Marine vulnerable at the worst possible time. Unfortunately, a flood of counterfeit electronic parts has made it a lot harder to prevent that from happening.

In March of 2011, the Senate Armed Services Committee initiated an investigation into counterfeit electronic parts in the Department of Defense (DOD) supply chain. The investigation uncovered overwhelming evidence of large numbers of counterfeit parts making their way into critical defense systems. It revealed failures by defense contractors and DOD to report counterfeit parts and gaps in DOD's knowledge of the scope and impact of such parts on defense systems. The investigation exposed a defense supply chain that relies on hundreds of unvetted independent distributors to supply electronic parts for some of our most sensitive defense systems. And, it found overwhelming evidence that companies in China are the primary source of counterfeit electronic parts in the defense supply chain.

During the Senate's consideration of the National Defense Authorization Act for Fiscal Year 2012, Chairman Carl Levin and Ranking Member John McCain offered an amendment to stop the importation of counterfeit electronic parts into the United States, address weaknesses in the defense supply chain, and to promote the adoption of aggressive counterfeit avoidance practices by DOD and the defense industry. The amendment was adopted in the Senate and a revised version was included in the final bill signed by President Barack Obama on December 31, 2011. The Committee's findings, described in this report, are stark evidence of the importance of the reforms contained in that law.

Flood of Counterfeits in Defense Supply Chain

The Committee's investigation found the problem of counterfeit parts to be widespread in the defense supply chain. Looking at just part of the supply chain over a two year period from 2009 to 2010, the investigation uncovered approximately 1,800 cases of suspect counterfeit electronic parts. The total number of individual suspect parts involved in those cases exceeded one million.

As to the source of those parts, the Committee tracked well over 100 of the approximately 1,800 cases of suspect counterfeit parts back through the supply chain. The vast majority of those trails led to China, with more than 70 percent of the suspect parts being traced to that country. U.S. government reports consistently point to China as the epicenter of the global trade in counterfeits. The Committee's findings provide overwhelming and undeniable evidence in support of that assessment.

All too often, counterfeit electronic parts from China end up in defense systems in the United States. In fact, the investigation uncovered dozens of examples of suspect counterfeit electronic parts in military systems, including on thermal weapons sights delivered to the Army, on mission computers for the Missile Defense Agency's Terminal High Altitude Area Defense (THAAD) missile, and on military aircraft including SH-60B, AH-64, and CH-46 helicopters and the C-17, C-130J, C-27J, and P-8A Poseidon. The Committee looked in-depth at three cases where suspect counterfeit parts from China made their way through the supply chain and into critical military systems.

- ### *Suspect Counterfeit Parts in the U.S. Navy SH-60B Helicopter*

The SH-60B is a Navy helicopter that conducts anti-submarine and anti-surface warfare, surveillance and targeting support. The SH-60B deploys on Navy cruisers, destroyers, and frigates and has a Forward Looking InfraRed or "FLIR" System which provides night vision capability. The FLIR also contains a laser used for targeting the SH-60B's hellfire missiles.

On September 8, 2011 the Raytheon Company alerted the U.S. Naval Supply Systems Command that electronic parts suspected to be counterfeit had been installed on three Electromagnetic Interference Filters (EIF) integrated into FLIR units delivered by Raytheon. While stating that the FLIR system is not "flight safety critical," the Navy has said that the failure of an EIF could cause the FLIR to fail and an SH-60B cannot conduct surface warfare missions involving its hellfire missiles without a functioning FLIR. A FLIR failure would also compromise the pilot's ability to avoid hazards and identify targets at night, limiting the SH-60B's ability to be deployed in night missions.

While three EIF that contained suspect parts were sold to Raytheon by a defense subcontractor in Texas, the Committee's investigation traced the parts though a complex supply chain that spanned four states and three countries, originating with a company called Huajie Electronics Ltd. in Shenzhen, China.

- ### *Suspect Counterfeit Parts in U.S. Air Force C-130J and C-27J*

The C-130J and C-27J are military cargo planes equipped with display units that provide the pilot with information on the health of the airplane, including engine status, fuel use, location, and warning messages. The display units are manufactured by L-3 Display Systems, a division of L-3 Communications. For the C-130J, L-3 Display Systems manufactures the display units for Lockheed Martin, the military's prime contractor for the C-130J. For the C-27J, L-3 Display Systems manufacturers the display units for Alenia Aeronautica (Alenia), a subcontractor to L-3 Integrated Systems, which is a separate division of L-3 Communications and the military's prime contractor for the C-27J.

In November 2010, L-3 Display Systems learned that a memory chip used in display units was suspect counterfeit. By that time, however, the company had already installed parts from the suspect lot in more than 500 display units, including in units intended for the C-27J, the Air Force's C-130J and C-17 aircraft, and the CH-46, a helicopter used by the Marine Corps. Failure of the memory chip could cause a display unit to show a degraded image, lose data, or even go blank. L-3 Display Systems informed its customer, Alenia, shortly after it discovered the problem. However, neither L-3 nor Alenia alerted the Air Force that the C-27Js were affected by the suspect part until September 19, 2011, nearly a year after it had been discovered.

L-3 Display Systems bought the suspect memory chips from an electronics distributor in California. That distributor, in turn, bought the chips from Hong Dark Electronic Trade, a company in Shenzhen, China. In addition to the suspect memory chips, the Committee's investigation revealed that in 2009 and 2010, L-3 Communications purchased tens of thousands of Hong Dark supplied electronic parts that entered the defense supply chain. According to the Air Force, "approximately 84,000 suspect counterfeit electronic parts purchased from Hong Dark entered the DOD supply chain, and many of these parts have been installed on DOD aircraft."

- ### *Suspect Counterfeit Parts in the Navy P-8A Poseidon*

The P-8A Poseidon is a Boeing 737 commercial airplane modified to incorporate antisubmarine and anti-surface warfare capabilities. As of October 2011, three P-8A flight test aircraft were in test at the Naval Air Station at Patuxent River, Maryland and the Navy intends to purchase 117 of the aircraft from Boeing.

On August 17, 2011, Boeing sent a message marked "Critical" to the Navy. The message said that an ice detection module installed on a P-8A test aircraft contained a "reworked part that should not have been put on the airplane originally and should be replaced immediately."

Boeing had first identified a problem with the part in December 2009 when an ice detection module failed on the company's flight line. In that case, the suspect part had literally fallen out of its socket and was found rattling around inside the module. An investigation by BAE Systems, which manufactures the module for Boeing, discovered that the part, and hundreds of others from the same lot, was a previously used part made to appear new. While BAE notified Boeing about the suspect parts in January 2010, it took Boeing more than a year and a half to notify the Navy.

BAE purchased the suspect parts from a company called Tandex Test Labs in California. Tandex, it turns out, failed to test most of the parts before selling them to BAE. The company had bought the parts from an independent distributor in Florida who, the Committee discovered, purchased them from an affiliate of A Access Electronics in Shenzhen, China.

Counterfeit Parts Drive Up Defense Costs

In addition to the safety and national security risks they create, counterfeit electronic parts also drive up the cost of defense systems. To cite just one example, in September 2010, the Missile Defense Agency (MDA) learned that mission computers for THAAD missiles contained suspect counterfeit memory devices. According to MDA, if the devices had failed, the THAAD missile itself would likely have failed.

The memory devices at issue were purchased by Honeywell from an independent distributor. Honeywell installed them on mission computers which it sold to Lockheed Martin. Lockheed, in turn, supplied them to MDA. Honeywell and Lockheed notified MDA when they figured out the parts were suspect and fixed the problem. But the cost of that fix, which MDA reimbursed to the two companies, was nearly $2.7 million. (In January 2012, MDA reported that Lockheed Martin's award fee on the THAAD contract was later reduced by $2.1 million as a result of the suspect counterfeit parts.)

Counterfeit electronic parts pose long-term reliability problems, and reliability is a major driver in the overall cost of a weapon system. According to the Department of Defense's Director of Operational Test and Evaluation:

> Poor reliability is a problem with major implications for cost . . . Unreliable systems have higher sustainment costs because, quite plainly, they break more frequently than planned. . . . Poor reliability leads to higher sustainment cost for replacement spares, maintenance, repair parts, facilities, staff, etc. Poor reliability hinders warfighter effectiveness and can essentially render weapons useless.

Keeping down operations and sustainment costs is important, since they account for about two-thirds of the overall lifecycle costs of major weapons systems.

Lack of Reporting Keeps Defense Industry Vulnerable

One way to avoid purchasing counterfeit parts is to know what parts are being counterfeited and which suppliers may be suspect. The Government-Industry Data Exchange Program (GIDEP) is a DOD program where government and industry participants can exchange information about counterfeit materials. GIDEP reports on suspect counterfeit electronic parts include information such as a part's manufacturer, the part number, and a description of characteristics that led to it being deemed suspect. Reports may also indicate who supplied the part. GIDEP members can review reports online through the program's website.

Raytheon's Vice-President for Supply Chain Operations testified to the Committee that sharing information through GIDEP "can help stop suppliers of counterfeit parts in their tracks." The Committee's investigation revealed, however, that reporting into GIDEP is severely lacking. While the Committee identified approximately 1,800 cases of suspect counterfeit parts in the defense supply chain in 2009 and 2010, only 271 total reports of suspect counterfeit parts were submitted to GIDEP during that period. The majority of those 271 reports were filed by just six companies. Only 13 GIDEP reports were filed by a government agency during that period.

New Law Aims to Clean Up Defense Supply Chain

The FY 2012 National Defense Authorization Act includes critically important provisions to address weaknesses in the defense supply chain that were identified in the Committee's investigation.

As described in detail in the full report, the overwhelming majority of suspect parts uncovered in the Committee's investigation did not originate in the United States. The NDAA contains provisions aimed at stopping counterfeit electronic parts before they enter the country. One of those provisions strengthens the inspection regime for imported electronic parts. Another ensures that the government can seek appropriate assistance from the private sector in determining whether or not an imported product is authentic.

Counterfeit parts often change hands many times before being purchased by defense contractors. The investigation revealed that contractors may know little about the ultimate source of the electronic parts they purchase. In fact, the Committee found that unvetted independent distributors are the source of the overwhelming majority of suspect parts in the defense supply chain. The 2012 NDAA includes provisions aimed at eliminating purchases from unknown and frequently suspect suppliers. It requires that electronic parts that are in production or available in stock be purchased from manufacturers or their authorized distributors. For parts that are out of production, the law requires DOD, defense contractors and subcontractors to buy from trusted suppliers.

Aggressive inspection and testing practices are also necessary to catch counterfeit parts that make it into the supply chain. The NDAA requires the Secretary of Defense to issue guidance on DOD acquisition policies and systems for the detection and avoidance of counterfeit electronic parts and requires the Secretary to implement a program requiring contractors to establish policies and procedures to address inspection and testing.

When suspect counterfeit parts are identified, they must be reported. Failing to do so allows suspect suppliers to operate with impunity and puts everyone at risk. The NDAA requires DOD and defense contractors who discover suspected counterfeit parts in a military system to report to appropriate government officials and GIDEP.

Finally, the government should not pay for counterfeit parts supplied by defense contractors and the 2012 NDAA ensures that does not happen. It requires the Secretary of Defense to issue regulations requiring that costs associated with remediating the use of counterfeit or suspect counterfeit parts in defense systems are paid by contractors who supplied them rather than the government. The new law strengthens the incentive for contractors to adopt aggressive counterfeit avoidance and detection programs and aligns DOD contracts with best practices in the commercial sector.

CONCLUSIONS OF THE SENATE ARMED SERVICES COMMITTEE

Source of Counterfeit Parts

Conclusion 1: *China is the dominant source country for counterfeit electronic parts that are infiltrating the defense supply chain.* The U.S. Trade Representative (USTR) has said that China's global manufacturing capacity "extends to all phases of the production and global distribution of counterfeit goods." The Committee's investigation uncovered overwhelming evidence that that is the case with electronic parts infiltrating the defense supply chain. The Committee tracked well over 100 cases of suspect counterfeit parts back through the supply chain. China was found to be the source country for suspect counterfeit parts in an overwhelming majority of those cases, with more than 70 percent of the suspect parts traced to that country. The next two largest source countries were the United Kingdom and Canada. The Committee identified instances in which both countries served as resale points for suspect counterfeit electronic parts from China.

Conclusion 2: *The Chinese government has failed to take steps to stop counterfeiting operations that are carried out openly in that country.* One Committee witness described visiting China and seeing public sidewalks covered with electronic components that had been harvested from e-waste. Another witness said he saw whole factories in China of 10,000 to 15,000 people set up for the purpose of counterfeiting. Counterfeit electronic parts are sold openly in public markets in China. Rather than acknowledging the problem and moving aggressively to shut down counterfeiters, the Chinese government has tried to avoid scrutiny, including denying visas to Committee staff to travel to mainland China as part of the Committee's investigation.

Department of Defense Actions on Counterfeits

Conclusion 3: *The Department of Defense lacks knowledge of the scope and impact of counterfeit parts on critical defense systems.* In a March 2010 report, the Government Accountability Office stated that "DOD is limited in its ability to determine the extent to which counterfeit parts exist in its supply chain." The Committee's findings support that statement. Reporting into the Government-Industry Data Exchange (GIDEP) program, which would allow DOD to track instances of counterfeit parts, is woefully lacking. During the period reviewed by the Committee, the Defense Logistics Agency (DLA), which is responsible for supplying DOD with most of its spare parts, neither consistently reported to GIDEP nor maintained a list of instances in which they had been supplied counterfeit electronic parts. And, in each of the three cases that the Committee investigated in depth, DOD was unaware that counterfeit electronic parts had been installed on certain defense systems until the Committee's investigation.

Conclusion 4: *The use of counterfeit electronic parts in defense systems can compromise performance and reliability, risk national security, and endanger the safety of military personnel.* The investigation uncovered dozens of examples of suspect counterfeit electronic parts in critical military systems, including on thermal weapons sights delivered to the Army, on mission computers for the Missile Defense Agency's Terminal High Altitude Area Defense (THAAD) missile, and on a large number of military airplanes. The potential impact of suspect parts on the performance and reliability of defense systems is significant. For example, according to MDA, if suspect counterfeit devices installed on the THAAD mission computers had failed, the THAAD missile itself would likely have failed. According to the Navy, had counterfeit parts contained in electromagnetic interference filters failed on an SH-60B helicopter, the aircraft's ability to conduct night missions and surface warfare missions involving hellfire missiles would have been compromised.

Conclusion 5: *Permitting contractors to recover costs incurred as a result of their own failure to detect counterfeit electronic parts does not encourage the adoption of aggressive counterfeit avoidance and detection programs.* Taxpayers should not be burdened with covering the costs of a contractor's failure to detect counterfeit electronic parts in its own supply chain. Moreover, government contracts that permit cost recovery in such circumstances contrast with agreements that some contractors enter into with their own suppliers. Raytheon's General Terms and Conditions relating to nonconforming material states that the "[c]ost of repair, rework, replacement, inspection, transportation, repackaging, and/or reinspection by Buyer shall be at Seller's expense." Similarly, BAE's General Provisions state that, in cases where a supplier delivers non-conforming work, BAE may "make, or have a third party make all repairs, modifications, or replacements necessary to enable work to comply in all respects with Contract requirements and charge the cost incurred to the SELLER."

Defense Industry

Conclusion 6: *The defense industry's reliance on unvetted independent distributors to supply electronic parts for critical military applications results in unacceptable risks to national security and the safety of U.S. military personnel.* The Committee identified approximately 1,800 cases of suspect counterfeit parts in the defense supply chain. Those parts were supplied by more than 650 companies, each of which relied on their own network of suppliers. DOD and defense contractors are frequently unaware of the ultimate source of electronic parts used in defense systems. The suspect counterfeit parts that were used in Electromagnetic Interference Filters (EIF) destined for the Navy's SH-60B helicopters, for example, changed hands five times before the parts were bought by the Raytheon subcontractor who built the EIFs. Those parts originated with Huajie Electronics in Shenzhen, China, a fact that neither DOD nor Raytheon was aware of prior to the Committee's investigation.

Conclusion 7: *Weaknesses in the testing regime for electronic parts create vulnerabilities that are exploited by counterfeiters.* The Committee reviewed test reports associated with the approximately 1,800 cases of suspect counterfeit parts identified in the investigation. Those reports reveal wide disparities in testing used by companies in the defense supply chain. Some companies require a range of testing; for example, exposing a part to aggressive solvents to determine whether markings are authentic or delidding part samples to examine their die. Other companies, however, are willing to accept parts that have only been subject to basic functional testing. The investigation also revealed deficiencies in the process used to determine whether and how parts are tested. For example, in the case of the counterfeit memory chips sold to L-3 Communications, the supplier in China selected and sent L-3 Communications' U.S.-based distributor a sample of 18 parts to test. Once those parts were tested and validated as authentic, the China-based supplier sold the company more than ten thousand of the chips. L-3's process at the time allowed the company to accept those chips without additional testing from an independent laboratory.

Conclusion 8: *The defense industry routinely failed to report cases of suspect counterfeit parts, putting the integrity of the defense supply chain at risk.* The vast majority of the approximately 1,800 cases of suspect counterfeit parts identified in the investigation appear to have gone unreported to DOD or criminal authorities. For example, in the case of the suspect counterfeit part contained in the Navy's P-8A airplane, Boeing failed to notify the Navy of the problem until the Committee began inquiring about the suspect counterfeits. Similarly, in the case of the suspect counterfeit memory chip contained in the C-27J, L-3 Communications did not notify the Air Force until the day before Committee staff was scheduled to meet with the Air Force program office responsible for that aircraft. Many cases also go unreported to the Government-Industry Data Exchange Program (GIDEP), a DOD program where government and industry participants can file reports about suspect counterfeits. While one industry witness told the Committee that sharing information on counterfeit parts through GIDEP "can help stop suppliers of counterfeit parts in their tracks," only 271 total reports were submitted to GIDEP during all of 2009 and 2010.

INTRODUCTION

Over the past few decades, U.S. defense systems have become increasingly dependent on electronic parts to enable their advanced capabilities. For example, the carrier-based variant of the Joint Strike Fighter, the U.S.'s next generation multi-role fighter, currently under development, contains more than 3,500 integrated circuits.[1] At the same time that our military systems have become more reliant on electronic parts, the market for those parts has changed dramatically, increasing the defense industry's vulnerability to counterfeits.

In some industries, the term "counterfeit" suggests an unauthorized copy of an authentic product. The definition of counterfeit adopted by DOD and a large segment of the defense industry, as it relates to electronic parts, includes both unauthorized copies and previously used parts that are made to look new, and are sold as new.[2] In January 2010, the Department of Commerce (DOC) published the results of a survey of the defense industrial base on counterfeit electronic parts.[3] The survey was initiated at the request of the U.S. Department of the Navy, Naval Air Systems Command (NAVAIR) based on its suspicion that "an increasing number of counterfeit/defective electronics were infiltrating the DOD supply chain and affecting weapon system reliability."[4] The results of the survey showed an alarming number of counterfeit instances, with the number growing from 3,868 in 2005 to 9,356 in 2008.[5]

DOC's survey was followed in March 2010 by a Government Accountability Office (GAO) report examining DOD's "knowledge of counterfeit parts in its supply chain" and "processes to detect and prevent counterfeit parts."[6] The report contains examples of counterfeit electronic parts in DOD's supply chain, including counterfeit integrated circuits used in F-15 flight control computers and counterfeit transistors used in systems for defeating shoulder-launched missiles.[7] GAO concluded that "DOD is limited in its ability to determine the extent to which counterfeit parts exist in its supply chain because it does not have a department-wide definition of the term 'counterfeit' and a consistent means to identify instances of suspected counterfeit parts."[8]

---

[1] Defense Advanced Research Projects Agency, *An analytical framework for cyber security* (November 2011).

[2] SAE Aerospace, *Aerospace Standard AS5553* (April 2004) at 8 (hereinafter "AS5553").

[3] U.S. Department of Commerce, Bureau of Industry and Security, Office of Technical Evaluation, *Defense Industrial Base Assessment: Counterfeit Electronics* (January 2010).

[4] *Ibid.* at i.

[5] *Ibid.* at i-ii. DOC surveyed 387 companies and organizations in the Department of Defense's (DOD) supply chain, including electronic part manufacturers, distributors, assemblers, defense contractors, and DOD agencies. The survey sought information on counterfeit electronic parts encountered by respondents from 2005 to 2008. DOC's survey sought information on discrete devices, integrated circuits, and circuit boards. *Ibid.* at i.

[6] GAO, *Defense Supplier Base Report: DOD Should Leverage Ongoing Initiatives in Developing Its Program to Mitigate Risk of Counterfeit Parts* (March 2010) at highlights page.

[7] *Ibid.* at 24.

[8] *Ibid.* at highlights page. In August 2009, DOD endorsed Aerospace Standard 5553, which contains a definition of counterfeit. However, according to GAO, "it is left to the discretion of each DOD program as to whether it wants to use the [SAE] standard." Some DOD officials told GAO that they were not even aware of the standard. *Ibid.* at 4. On December 14, 2011 DOD issued Department of Defense Instruction (DODI) 4140.01 DOD Supply Chain Materiel Management Policy. The DODI defines "counterfeit materiel" as "[m]ateriel whose identity or

In January 2011, the Committee initiated an investigation to fill in gaps in what is known about the scope and impact of counterfeit electronic parts in the defense supply chain. The Committee sought documents and information on: specific incidents of counterfeit electronic parts; the risks and costs associated with counterfeit electronic parts; the source of those counterfeits; and DOD's knowledge of and response to incidents of counterfeit electronic parts. In the course of its investigation, the Committee reviewed more than 100,000 pages of documents from DOD, electronic part manufacturers, defense contractors and subcontractors, laboratories that test electronic parts, and electronic part distributors. Staff also met with and interviewed dozens of individuals. This report documents the Committee's findings.

Counterfeit electronic parts pose a threat not only to national security but also to the defense industry. The Department of Defense and DOD contractors share a common interest in eliminating that threat and both DOD and its contractors cooperated with the Committee's investigation.

The report consists of five sections. Section I provides background on counterfeiting and discusses factors that make defense systems particularly vulnerable to counterfeit electronic parts. Section II describes the Committee's findings on the extent of counterfeiting in the defense supply chain and discusses the types of parts and countries of origin of counterfeit parts identified by the Committee. Section III describes an investigation, conducted by GAO at the Committee's request, into online sales of counterfeit parts. Section IV consists of several case studies of counterfeit electronic parts that were identified by the Committee as having been integrated into defense systems. Section V discusses suspect parts identified by the Defense Logistics Agency (DLA) and describes agency policies and practices relating to counterfeit parts. Section VI describes provisions contained in the FY 2012 National Defense Authorization Act aimed at reducing the number of counterfeit electronic parts in the defense supply chain.

---

characteristics have been deliberately misrepresented, falsified, or altered without legal right to do so." Department of Defense, *Instruction 4140.01: DOD Supply Chain Materiel Management Policy* (December 14, 2011) at 17.

I.   The Impact of Counterfeit Parts on the Defense Supply Chain

A. Background on Counterfeits

According to a January 2010 report published by the Department of Commerce (DOC), the number of counterfeit incidents in the defense supply chain increased dramatically, growing from 3,868 in 2005 to 9,356 in 2008.[9] That growth reflects broader trends in counterfeiting. In April 2011, the United States Trade Representative (USTR) reported that counterfeiting "has evolved in recent years from a localized industry concentrated on copying high-end designer goods to a sophisticated global business involving the mass production and sale of a vast array of fake goods."[10] U.S. Department of Homeland Security (DHS) data on goods seized at the border for violations of intellectual property rights reflects that growth, indicating a more than 400 percent increase in the number of seizures between 2002 and 2011.[11]

While it is difficult to quantify the economic impact of counterfeiting on the U.S. economy, according to GAO, "research in specific industries suggests that the problem is sizeable, which is of particular concern as many U.S. industries are leaders in the creation of intellectual property."[12] USTR reports that intellectual property infringement "causes significant financial losses for rights holders and legitimate businesses" and "undermines key U.S. comparative advantages in innovation and creativity to the detriment of American businesses and workers."[13] With respect to counterfeit semiconductors, the Semiconductor Industry Association (SIA) estimates that counterfeits cost U.S. semiconductor companies more than $7.5 billion annually in lost revenue, a figure SIA says results in the loss of nearly 11,000 American jobs.[14]

B. Source Countries of Counterfeits

While counterfeiting occurs in many countries, China is the primary source of the problem. In fiscal year 2011 alone, China was the source of more than 80 percent of the total number of seizures for violations of intellectual property rights. The value of those seizures

---

[9] U.S. Department of Commerce, Bureau of Industry and Security, Office of Technical Evaluation, *Defense Industrial Base Assessment: Counterfeit Electronics* (January 2010) at i-ii.

[10] United States Trade Representative, *2011 Special 301 Report* (April 2011) at 9-10.

[11] U.S. Customs and Border Protection, U.S. Immigration and Customs Enforcement, *Intellectual Property Rights Fiscal Year 2011 Seizure Statistics – Final Report* (January 2012) at 7.

[12] GAO, *Intellectual Property: Observations on Efforts to Quantify the Economic Effects of Counterfeit and Pirated Goods* (April 2010) at 15-16. According to the GAO study "the illicit nature of counterfeiting and piracy makes estimating the economic impact of IP infringements extremely difficult, so assumptions must be used to offset the lack of data. Efforts to estimate losses involve assumptions such as the rate at which consumers would substitute counterfeit for legitimate products, which can have enormous impacts on the resulting estimates. Because of the significant differences in types of counterfeited and pirated goods and industries involved, no single method can be used to develop estimates. Each method has limitations, and most experts observed that it is difficult, if not impossible, to quantify the economy-wide impacts." *Ibid.* at highlights page.

[13] United States Trade Representative, *2011 Special 301 Report* (April 2011) at 5.

[14] Hearing to Receive Information Relative to the Committee's Investigation Into Counterfeit Electronic Parts in the Department of Defense Supply Chain, Senate Armed Services Committee (November 8, 2011) at 39 (hereinafter "SASC Hearing").

amounted to over 80 percent of the domestic value of all seizures made that year.[15] By comparison, Turkey was second on the list for the number of seizures in 2011 with less than 5 percent of the total. India was second on the list for value of goods seized at only 3 percent.[16] According to DHS data, for each of the ten years leading up to 2010, China has been the top source country, in terms of the value of goods seized for violations of intellectual property rights.[17]

In April 2011, USTR issued its annual "Special 301" report reviewing the global state of intellectual property rights. The USTR report contains a Priority Watch List of countries where "particular problems exist" for the protection of intellectual property.[18] While twelve countries appear on that list, the report dedicated special attention to China, stating that the country's global manufacturing capacity "extends to all phases of the production and global distribution of counterfeit goods."[19]

In December 2011, USTR issued its "Notorious Markets List," which identifies markets that are "reportedly engaged in piracy and counterfeiting."[20] China is home to four of the 15 notorious physical markets on the list.[21] The previous list, issued in February 2011, listed 17 "notorious" physical markets. Of those 17, China is home to five.[22] China is the only country on either list identified as being home to more than one notorious physical market.

For its report on counterfeit electronic parts in the defense supply chain, the Department of Commerce asked survey respondents to identify countries suspected or confirmed to be the source of counterfeit electronic components. Respondents named China as a source of counterfeits more than four and a half times more frequently than any other country.[23]

In meetings with Committee staff, defense officials, semiconductor manufacturers, defense contractors and electronic part distributors all identified China as the primary source of counterfeit electronic components. The Committee's findings support their assessment. As discussed in more depth below, the Committee tracked well over 100 specific instances of

---

[15] U.S. Customs and Border Protection, U.S. Immigration and Customs Enforcement, *Intellectual Property Rights Fiscal Year 2011 Seizure Statistics – Final Report* (January 2012) at Table 6. While CBP and ICE data identify Hong Kong and mainland China separately, the Committee's report combines the two.
[16] *Ibid.* at Table 6.
[17] U.S. Customs and Border Protection, U.S. Immigration and Customs Enforcement, *Intellectual Property Rights Fiscal Year 2010 Seizure Statistics – Final Report* (January 2011) at 10.
[18] United States Trade Representative, *2011 Special 301 Report* (April 2011) at 45.
[19] The USTR also stated, "According to industry reports, the range of goods counterfeited in China includes apparel and footwear, mobile phones, pharmaceuticals and medical equipment, herbal remedies, wine and liquor, other beverages, agricultural chemicals, electronic components, computer and networking equipment, software and related products, batteries, cigarettes, cosmetics, home appliances, cement, and auto parts, as well as merchandise based on copyrighted works." *Ibid.* at 21.
[20] United States Trade Representative, *Out-of-Cycle Review of Notorious Markets* (December 20, 2011) at 1.
[21] Other countries who are home to physical markets included on the list were Ecuador, Paraguay, Indonesia, Argentina, India, Ukraine, Philippines, Thailand, Colombia, Mexico, and Pakistan. *Ibid.* at 5-6.
[22] Other countries who are home to physical markets included on the list were Ecuador, Paraguay, Indonesia, Argentina, India, Ukraine, Philippines, Thailand, Colombia, Mexico, Russia, and Pakistan. United States Trade Representative, *Out of Cycle Review of Notorious Markets* (February 28, 2011) at 3-5.
[23] U.S. Department of Commerce, Bureau of Industry and Security, Office of Technical Evaluation, *Defense Industrial Base Assessment: Counterfeit Electronics* (January 2010) at 177-78.

suspect counterfeit electronic parts backward through the supply chain.[24] More than 70 percent of the suspect parts were traced back to China.

The Committee attempted to send staff to mainland China to meet with electronic part manufacturers and distributors and visit public markets where counterfeit electronic parts are reportedly sold. On May 12, 2011, Chairman Levin wrote to the Chinese Ambassador to the United States, informing him of the planned trip and advising him that the visit was part of the Committee's investigation.[25] In response to the letter, an official from the Chinese Embassy told Committee staff that the issues under investigation by the Committee were "sensitive" and that if the results of the investigation were not positive, it could be "damaging" to the U.S.-China relationship.[26]

Committee staff submitted visa applications to the Chinese Embassy, but those applications were not acted upon. On June 7, 2011, Chairman Levin and Ranking Member McCain wrote to the Chinese Ambassador asking for his personal assistance in resolving the visa issue.[27] In response, the Chinese Embassy suggested that the trip be postponed to an undetermined date and advised the Committee that if a visit were allowed to go forward, it was the Chinese government's practice to have a government official attend meetings between Committee staff and private companies in the country. The Committee was unwilling to accept that condition and the visas were not approved.

In June, staff members traveled to Hong Kong, where a visa is not required, and again sought entry into mainland China. Appeals on the Committee's behalf from the most senior U.S. diplomats in Hong Kong and Beijing were unsuccessful, and the staff members were refused entry into mainland China.

C. How Counterfeit Electronic Parts Are Made

Much of the material used to make counterfeit electronic parts is electronic waste or "e-waste" shipped from the United States and the rest of the world to China. In fact, the Department of Commerce (DOC) reported that e-waste has "turned into an abundance of discrete electronic components and microcircuits for counterfeit parts."[28] E-waste enters the country through the Port of Hong Kong where it is often placed on trucks and hauled to cities like Shantou in Guangdong Province.[29] USTR says that many counterfeiting activities in China can be traced to Guangdong Province.[30]

---

[24] In the defense industry, the term "suspect counterfeit" is used in one of two ways. First, it is common to use the terms "suspect counterfeit" and "counterfeit" interchangeably. In the absence of explicit confirmation from the original manufacturer of the chip about the authenticity of the part, defense contractors have expressed a preference to use the term suspect counterfeit over counterfeit. Second, where a sample of parts from a delivery (called a "lot") displays evidence of counterfeiting, the entire lot is considered to be suspect counterfeit.

[25] Letter from Senator Carl Levin to His Excellency Zhang Yesui (May 12, 2011).

[26] Committee Staff telephone conversation with Ms. Fei Lu (May 16, 2011).

[27] Letter from Senators Carl Levin and John McCain to His Excellency Zhang Yesui (June 7, 2011).

[28] U.S. Department of Commerce Bureau of Industry and Security Office of Technical Evaluation, *Defense Industrial Base Assessment: Counterfeit Electronics* (January 2010) at 74.

[29] Committee Staff meetings and interviews, *see e.g.*, Committee Staff meeting with Thomas Sharp (January 11, 2011).

[30] United States Trade Representative, *2011 Special 301 Report* (April 2011) at 21.

Once in Guangdong, e-waste may be disassembled by hand, washed in dirty rivers, and dried on city sidewalks. Thomas Sharpe, the president of an independent electronic parts distributor and testing laboratory used by many defense contractors, told the Committee about what he saw when he visited Shantou's counterfeiting district in 2008:

> While there, I witnessed e-scrap piled outside of buildings throughout large areas of the town, throughout the outskirts of the town, used electronic parts being washed in a river, and laid on the riverbank to dry, nylon sacks with harvested components being dumped onto sidewalks and sorted by women and children, laid out there for the monsoon rains of July to wash them naturally, cardboard and plastic bins filled with expensive brand name components and harvested from scrap printed circuit boards ready for processing. [31]

Once they have been washed, parts may be sanded down to remove the existing part number and other marks that indicate a part's quality or performance. In many cases, the date code, a series of numbers on an electronic part that indicates when it was manufactured, is changed to make the part appear newer than it is. In a process known as "black topping," the tops of the parts may be recoated to hide sanding marks. State-of-the-art printing equipment may be used to put false markings on the parts. Once they have been through the counterfeiting process, the parts are packaged and shipped to Shenzhen (also in Guangdong Province) or other cities to be sold in markets or over the Internet. [32]

Components harvested from e-waste are not the only type of counterfeit. The semiconductor industry reports that it has "found factories that manufacture blank chips on which counterfeit markings are added later in a made-to-order fashion." [33] Vivek Kamath, Raytheon's Vice-President of Supply Chain Operations, described his experience in China before his employment by Raytheon, stating that he saw "whole factories" set up for counterfeiting and employing 10,000 to 15,000 people. [34] Kamath said, "the amazing thing about the whole thing is it's very open. There is nothing discreet about it. And it's just almost as if it's just accepted as another business model in the country." [35]

The conditions under which counterfeit electronic components are processed stand in stark contrast to the production methods of legitimate manufacturers. Semiconductor companies spend billions of dollars to protect their product from exposure to conditions that are commonplace in the counterfeiting business. A recent Department of Justice filing in a case involving counterfeit electronic parts described conditions in a state-of-the-art semiconductor manufacturing facility:

> [T]he air in a semiconductor fabrication plant "clean room" is 1000 times cleaner than that found in a hospital operating room, because even a tiny particle of dust

---

[31] SASC Hearing at 16.
[32] Committee Staff meetings and interviews.
[33] SASC Hearing at 35.
[34] Committee Staff interview of Vivek Kamath (October 6, 2011) at 74.
[35] *Ibid.* at 74-75.

can negatively impact a device. . . . Fabrication plant workers wear special clothing, head-to-toe, designed to minimize [electro-static discharge]. The clothing is colloquially referred to as a "bunny suit." . . . [R]obotics are also utilized to minimize [electro-static discharge] . . . [S]ince vibration can negatively impact production, entire plants are built on intricate shock absorption systems so that even vibrations from the flow of cars on nearby roads is minimized. Because moisture can harm the devices, special storage and shipping packaging is used to keep the devices moisture-free.[36]

Although counterfeiters often use crude methods to harvest components for counterfeiting, it does not mean that counterfeiters are unsophisticated or that counterfeit electronic parts are easy to identify. In fact, Thomas Sharpe told the Committee that "[m]any of the current counterfeiting techniques are already beyond the in-house detection capabilities of most open-market suppliers."[37] The increasing sophistication of counterfeiters is posing significant challenges to the defense industry's ability to detect them. According to Raytheon's Vice-President of Supply Chain Operations:

[W]hat keeps us up at night is the dynamic nature of this threat because by the time we've figured out how to test for these counterfeits, they've figured out how to get around it. And it's literally on almost a daily basis they change and the sophistication of the counterfeiting is amazing to us. We're finding that you have to go down to the microns to be able to figure out that it's actually a counterfeit.[38]

D. Why Counterfeit Electronic Parts Are Dangerous

Counterfeit electronic parts pose a significant risk to the performance of defense systems. Even if counterfeits made from previously used parts and salvaged from e-waste may initially perform, there is no way to predict how well they will perform, how long they will last, and the full impact of failure. As Samsung, a major semiconductor manufacturer, put it, "[s]emiconductor components have limited useful lives."[39] Xilinx, another semiconductor manufacturer, described the risks of using parts salvaged from e-waste:

The devices may have been reclaimed and potentially exposed to excessive heat in order to dismount them from a circuit board. These cases pose a significant reliability risk owing to the potential exposure to excessive heat and electro-static discharge (ESD) damage. . . . With respect to ESD, there are many potential damage mechanisms that could have affected the devices. Some of these could be catastrophic; others may create a damage mechanism that is latent for an undetermined amount of time. . . . Though the devices may initially function, it

---

[36] Government's Consolidated Memorandum in Aid of Sentencing and Motion for Downward Departure Pursuant to U.S.S.G. § 5K1.1, United States District Court for the District of Columbia (September 9, 2011) at 7-8 (hereinafter "McCloskey Sentencing Memorandum").

[37] SASC Hearing at 17.

[38] Committee Staff interview of Vivek Kamath (October 6, 2011) at 11.

[39] Letter from Terrence H. Cross, Vice President and General Counsel, Samsung Electronics, to Senators Carl Levin and John McCain (November 7, 2011).

would be next to impossible to predict what amount of life is remaining, or what damage may have been caused to the circuitry.[40]

A second danger associated with counterfeit electronic parts has to do with how they are marked. The marking on an electronic part includes information that allows a buyer to determine its performance grade. Knowing a part's performance grade is critical as military grade parts, for example, are certified to operate over a broader temperature range than industrial or commercial grade parts. As a result, military grade parts may be used when a device is expected to be exposed to extreme conditions, such as in defense applications. Counterfeiters, however, often remove the original manufacturer's marking on a part and remark it with an entirely different part number. So, while a part may be of commercial grade it could be remarked as military grade. Such remarked parts may pass basic testing but fail in the field when they are exposed to extreme temperatures and other conditions.[41]

The President of the Semiconductor Industry Association likened using counterfeit parts to "playing Russian roulette," explaining, "[w]ith luck, the chip will not function at all and will be discovered in testing. But in some cases the chip may work for a while, but because of the environmental abuse it could fail at a critical time – when the product containing the chip is stressed – as in combat."[42]

Contractors conduct acceptance testing of defense systems where the systems may be subjected to heat, vibration and other stresses. However, such testing may not weed out all counterfeit parts. According to General Patrick O'Reilly, the Director of the Missile Defense Agency (MDA):[43]

> A counterfeit part may pass all production testing. However, it is possible that the part was damaged during unauthorized processing (e.g., removing the part from a previous assembly, or sanding the surface in order to place a new part number) causing the deployed system to fail. Similarly, reliability may be affected because a counterfeit part may be near the end of its useful life when it is installed. Should any mission critical component fail, that system fails and national security is impacted.[44]

E. The Defense Industry's Vulnerability to Counterfeit Electronic Parts

Over the past few decades, defense systems have become increasingly dependent on electronic parts to enable their advanced capabilities.[45] Over the same period of time, the

---

[40] Letter from Moshe Gavrielov, President and CEO, Xilinx, to Senators Carl Levin and John McCain (October 26, 2011).

[41] McCloskey Sentencing Memorandum at 3, 7, 12.

[42] SASC Hearing at 39.

[43] *Ibid.* at 73.

[44] Hearing to Receive Testimony on Ballistic Missile Defense Policies and Programs in Review of the Defense Authorization Request for Fiscal Year 2012 and the Future Years Defense Program, LTG Patrick J. O'Reilly answers to questions for the record (April 13, 2011).

[45] Ted J. Glum, 2008 Common Defense Conference (September 3, 2008).

electronic parts market has changed dramatically, increasing the defense industry's vulnerability to counterfeits.

When an electronic part is no longer economical to produce due to declining demand, manufacturers stop making it. It has become increasingly common for parts used to build or sustain defense systems to become obsolete. In fact, according to a 2004 Defense Science Board study, "[i]n many cases, components procurement officials for *new* DOD production systems find that the [integrated circuits] incorporated in their designs are at or nearing the end of life and are about to be out of production."[46] Two reasons for the defense industry's reliance on such parts are a weakening of the industry's influence in the semiconductor market and the shrinking production lifecycle of electronic parts.

With respect to the defense industry's market influence, according to the Director of the DOD's Microelectronics Activity (DMEA), in the 1980s, the defense industry made up 26 percent of the demand for semiconductors. However, by 2008, that figure had dropped to 0.1 percent.[47]

As the defense industry's market influence has waned, production life cycles for electronic parts have shrunk considerably. An individual part may now only be in production for 18 months or two years. According to IHS Inc., a company that monitors notifications of electronic components that go out of production, nearly 800,000 such notices have been issued for integrated circuits in the past ten years.[48]

The combination of the defense industry's waning market influence and the shrinking production lifecycles for semiconductors is challenging DOD's ability to build and sustain systems that are often expected to operate for decades. The Department of Commerce (DOC) described the challenge:

> Systems such as the F-15, which was put into service in 1975 and is scheduled to be in service well beyond 2010, are used far after their original end-of-life projections. This is as opposed to the projected lifecycles of electronic parts and components produced by industry, which can be as brief as two years. Thus, DOD procurement agents quickly find their multiple sources of needed electronic parts turning into sole sources or disappearing altogether. This problem has been further compounded by extended usage of weapon systems and platforms in Iraq and Afghanistan, which have diminished existing and well intentioned life of type or life time buys and spare parts inventories.[49]

While obsolescence is not unique to electronic parts, that is where the problem is most acute. In fact, according to DMEA, more than 90 percent of all DOD obsolescence cases are

---

[46] Defense Science Board Task Force, *High Performance Microchip Supply* (February 2005) at 35 (emphasis added).

[47] Ted J. Glum, 2008 Common Defense Conference (September 3, 2008).

[48] IHS data on end of life notices for integrated circuits provided in response to Committee request (January 27, 2012).

[49] U.S. Department of Commerce Bureau of Industry and Security Office of Technical Evaluation, *Defense Industrial Base Assessment: Counterfeit Electronics* (January 2010) at 1.

electronic parts.[50] DMEA's Director summarized it this way, "The defense community is critically reliant on a technology that obsoletes itself every 18 months, is made in unsecure locations and over which we have absolutely no market share influence."[51]

F. The Defense Industry and the Independent Distribution Market

When an electronic part is no longer available from the manufacturer or a manufacturer's authorized distributor, buyers are often forced to rely on independent distributors to supply the part. There are thousands of companies that act as independent electronic parts distributors in the United States alone.[52] Globally, the number is thought to be significantly higher.[53]

Buying parts in the independent distribution market can present significant risks. Some independent distributors hold significant stocks of parts and make counterfeit avoidance and detection programs a priority in their businesses.[54] Others may hold no stock, simply act as parts brokers, and conduct little or no testing of the parts they buy and sell.[55] There are also companies, many of which are located in China, that are in the business of selling counterfeit parts.[56] The Committee's own findings, described in greater detail below, found that virtually all of the suspect counterfeit parts tracked through the defense supply chain during the investigation were supplied by independent distributors.

One way to mitigate the risk of obtaining counterfeit parts from independent distributors is to audit potential distributors and develop a list of trusted suppliers.[57] MDA performs site assessments of independent distributors and audits past performance in determining whether to approve them as a source of electronic parts.[58] The results of MDA's assessments demonstrate why that practice is so critical.

As of November 2011, MDA had conducted inspections of 51 independent distributors. According to MDA's Director, Lieutenant General Patrick O'Reilly, "more than 60 percent [of those 51 independent distributors] were assessed as moderate to high risk for providing counterfeit products."[59] MDA even found independent distributors that engaged in "deceptive marketing" by posting photos of fake facilities on their website to appear more established or to

---

[50] Ted J. Glum, 2008 Common Defense Conference (September 3, 2008).

[51] *Ibid.*

[52] IC Source and netComponents are two companies that operate Internet-based trading platforms for electronic parts. On February 2, 2012, IC Source's web site stated that the company has 3,000 members. IC Source describes itself as a "global leader among information clearinghouses for the electronic components brokering industry." IC Source Website, *available at* http://www.icsource.com (last visited January 11, 2011). netComponents advised the Committee that it is aware of approximately 1,600 independent distributors in the United States. Email from Nigel Larsen to Joe Bryan (February 2, 2012).

[53] *See, e.g.,* IDEA, Introduction to the Open Market (December 10, 2010).

[54] The Independent Distributors of Electronics Association (IDEA), a non-profit trade association representing independent distributors, requires prospective members to demonstrate that they adhere to IDEA-STD-1010, which contains requirements for the inspection of electronic parts bought on the open market. However, only 34 independent distributors are members of IDEA. Email from Debra Eggeman to Joe Bryan (January 16, 2012).

[55] *See, generally,* documents received in response to Committee requests to independent distributors.

[56] *See, e.g.,* discussion of electronic part suppliers in McCloskey Sentencing Memorandum at 33.

[57] *See, e.g.,* Committee Staff interview of Vivek Kamath (October 6, 2011) at 28, 33-34; SASC Hearing at 74-76.

[58] SASC Hearing at 74-76.

[59] *Ibid.* at 73.

misrepresent the size of their operations.[60] One independent distributor even listed its address as a corporate building when, in reality, the company's "facility" was a local United Parcel Service store.[61]

[60] MDA, *MDA Information Briefing to the Senate Armed Services Committee on Counterfeit Parts* (December 15, 2010) at 4.
[61] *Ibid.*

II.   Committee-Identified Suspect Counterfeit Parts

The Committee initiated its investigation to determine the extent and impact of counterfeit electronic parts in the defense supply chain. In February 2011, the Committee asked the Defense Logistics Agency (DLA) to provide a list of suspect counterfeit electronic parts identified by DLA in 2009 and 2010, the names of the companies that supplied the parts, and other information. DLA is the DOD agency that supplies more than 80 percent of the military's spare parts, including electronic parts.[62] That same month, the Committee sent letters to ten large Department of Defense contractors asking for information on suspect counterfeit electronic parts intended for use in a DOD system or subsystem that the contractors had identified in calendar years 2009 and 2010.[63]

The Committee also asked contractors for the names of companies that performed testing of electronic parts. In response to that request, the contractors identified more than 350 companies that performed testing of electronic parts for them.[64] The Committee identified 22 companies that each conducted testing for at least three of the defense contractors. The Committee then requested information on counterfeit or suspect counterfeit electronic parts identified by those 22 testers in 2009 and 2010.[65]

The requests to DLA, defense contractors, and testers generated information on more than 1,800 cases involving suspect counterfeit electronic parts. DLA reported more than 200 cases,[66] contractors reported more than 150 cases, and testers reported approximately 1,500 cases. The total number of individual suspect parts involved in those approximately 1,800 cases exceeds one million.[67]

---

[62] Defense Logistics Agency Website, *available at* http://www.dla.mil/Pages/ataglance.aspx (last visited February 22, 2012).

[63] The letter also asked for part numbers, the name of the supplier, a description of the intended use for the part, why the parts were suspect counterfeit, whether or not the contractor had reported the suspect parts to the Government Industry Data Exchange Program (GIDEP) or ERAI (a privately-run database that tracks counterfeit parts), and how the parts were ultimately disposed. *See, e.g.,* Letter from Senators Carl Levin and John McCain to Linda Parker Hudson (February 18, 2011).

[64] The nine contractors were: The Boeing Company, Raytheon Company, Lockheed Martin Corporation, Science Applications International Corporation (SAIC), Northrup Grumman Corporation, L-3 Communications Corporation, General Dynamics Corporation, ITT Corporation, and BAE Systems.

[65] The Committee also asked for the total number of electronic parts those testers had determined to be suspect counterfeit during the relevant period; copies of testing reports for suspect parts; and the basis for the determination that parts were suspect counterfeit.

[66] DLA actually reported 381 incidents. However, the agency did not provide detailed information on 130 incidents it deemed "law enforcement sensitive." In addition, DLA identified many electronic parts that were not integrated circuits or discrete devices. The Committee's analysis focuses on the 202 cases that involved integrated circuits and discrete devices and were not deemed law enforcement sensitive.

[67] While the combined total of incidents reported exceeds 1,800, the Committee is using the figure of "approximately 1800" because some incidents were reported by more than one respondent. In addition, DLA's response included incidents from the first quarter of 2011. Defense Logistics Agency answers to February 18, 2011 written questions from Committee Staff (May 19, 2011).

A. *Country of Origin of SASC-Identified Suspect Counterfeit Parts*

1. Country of Origin for First-Tier Distributors

The Committee reviewed documentation relating to each of the approximately 1,800 cases to determine the country of origin of the more than 650 companies that supplied parts.[68] Virtually all of those 650 companies ("first-tier suppliers") were independent electronic parts distributors. In all but a few cases, the Committee was able to determine the country in which first-tier distributors were based. As reflected in Figure 1, almost 80 percent were either located in or had a business presence in the United States while 20 percent had no business presence in the United States.

Figure 1

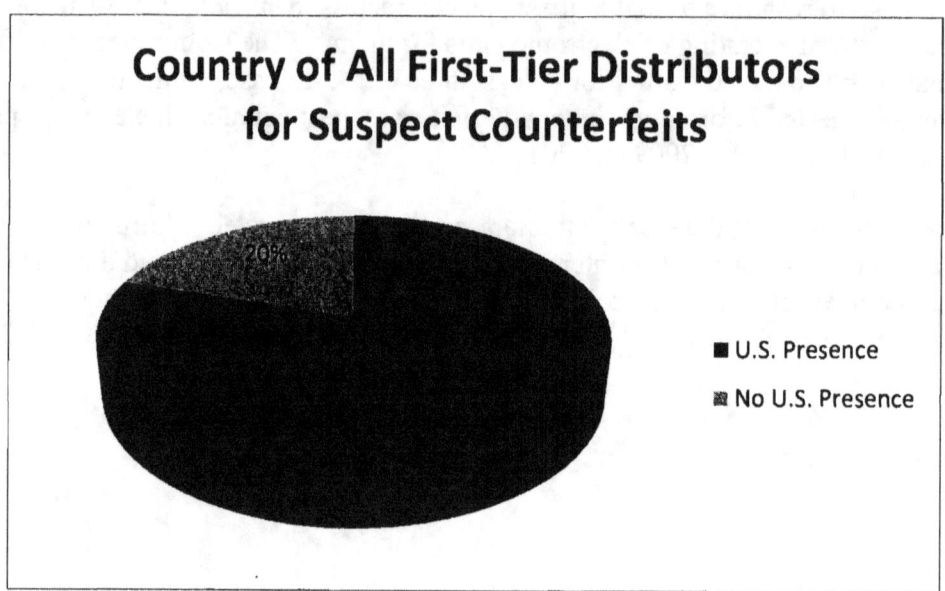

As reflected in Figure 2, of the 20 percent of first-tier distributors that had no U.S. presence, China-based companies made up the largest portion at 44 percent of the total. The next most common home countries for distributors that lacked a U.S. presence were Canada and the U.K., respectively. As discussed below, the Committee's investigation identified instances where both of those countries served as resale points for counterfeit parts purchased from suppliers in China.

---

[68] In many cases identified by testing companies, the testers had been hired by independent distributors who were not attempting to sell counterfeit parts but rather were seeking to determine the authenticity of parts that they had purchased or were planning to purchase.

Figure 2

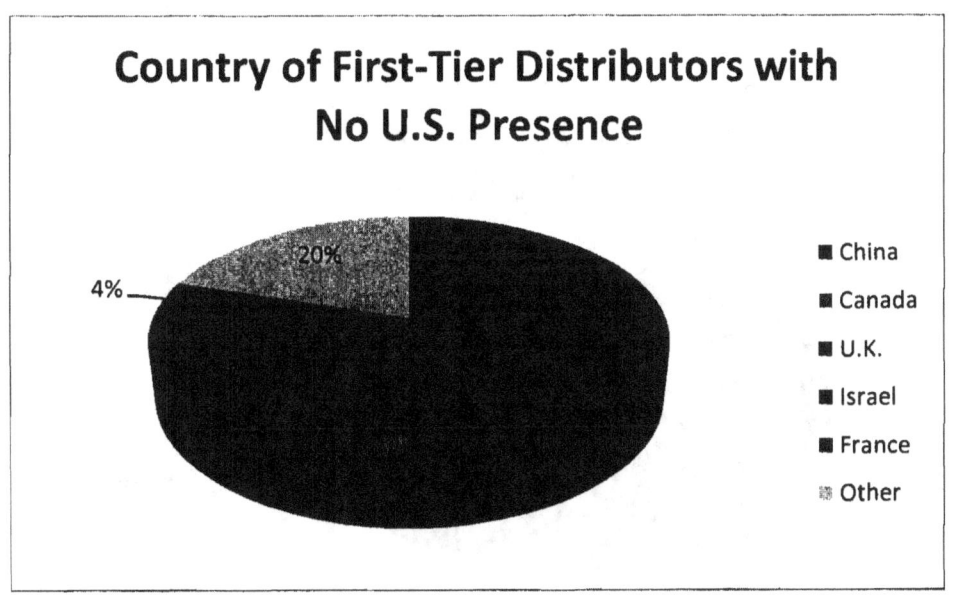

Country of First-Tier Distributors with No U.S. Presence

- China
- Canada
- U.K.
- Israel
- France
- Other

2. <u>Country of Origin for Parts Tracked Back Through the Supply Chain</u>

To determine the ultimate source of counterfeit parts, the Committee tracked 126 of the approximately 1,800 cases back through the supply chain. Each of the 126 cases was associated with a purchase or planned purchase by an independent distributor located in the United States. The Committee asked those U.S.-based first-tier distributors to identify the company that supplied them with the suspect counterfeit parts ("second-tier distributor").[69] Based on that information, the Committee posed the same question to the U.S.-based second-tier distributors. That exercise was repeated for subsequent tiers in the supply chain until a part was traced to a supplier outside the United States.

Figure 3 reflects the breakdown of countries to which the 126 cases were ultimately traced. China was found to be the source country for suspect counterfeit parts in an overwhelming majority of the 126 cases, with more than 70 percent of the suspect parts traced to that country. The next two largest source countries were the United Kingdom (UK) and Canada, with 11 percent and 9 percent of cases being tracked to those two countries, respectively. The Committee identified instances in which both countries served as resale points for suspect counterfeit electronic parts from China.[70]

---

[69] The Committee also asked distributors for information about the disposition of the suspect counterfeit parts, i.e., whether the parts were destroyed, returned to the second tier distributor, or resold to another customer.

[70] As described in Section IV, the Committee traced suspect counterfeit parts contained in electromagnetic interference filters purchased by the U.S. Navy for use on SH-60B helicopters to Pivotal Electronics, a UK-based company. Pivotal Electronics purchased the suspect counterfeits from Huajie Electronics Ltd. in Shenzhen, China. The Committee also identified seven China-based suppliers who sold suspect counterfeit parts to Liberty Electronics (2000), Inc. in Ontario, Canada.

Figure 3

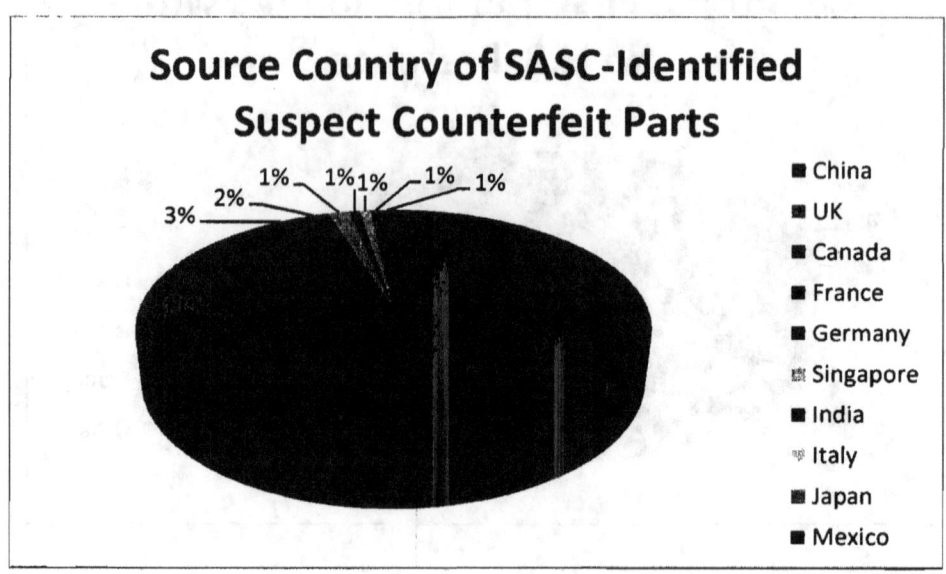

B. Part Characteristics of SASC-Identified Suspect Counterfeit Parts

In addition to identifying the country of origin for suspect counterfeit parts, the Committee sent the full list of 1,800 manufacturer part numbers with lot date codes to Missile Defense Agency's (MDA) Quality and Safety Parts and Materials Advisory Group (PMAG) personnel at the Naval Surface Warfare Center Crane (NSWC-Crane), and asked for information on the obsolescence status and performance grade of the parts.[71] NSWC-Crane maintains lifecycle information on electronic parts used in defense systems in order to alert DOD and defense contractors about parts that are about to become obsolete.

1. Production Status of Suspect Counterfeit Parts

MDA was able to determine the production status of more than 1,500 of the part numbers provided by the Committee. As reflected in Figure 4, of those 1,500 part numbers, approximately 70 percent were no longer in production as of May 2011. The remaining 30 percent were parts still in production.

---

[71] Letter from Senators Carl Levin and John McCain to Frederick Schipp (May 24, 2011).

Figure 4

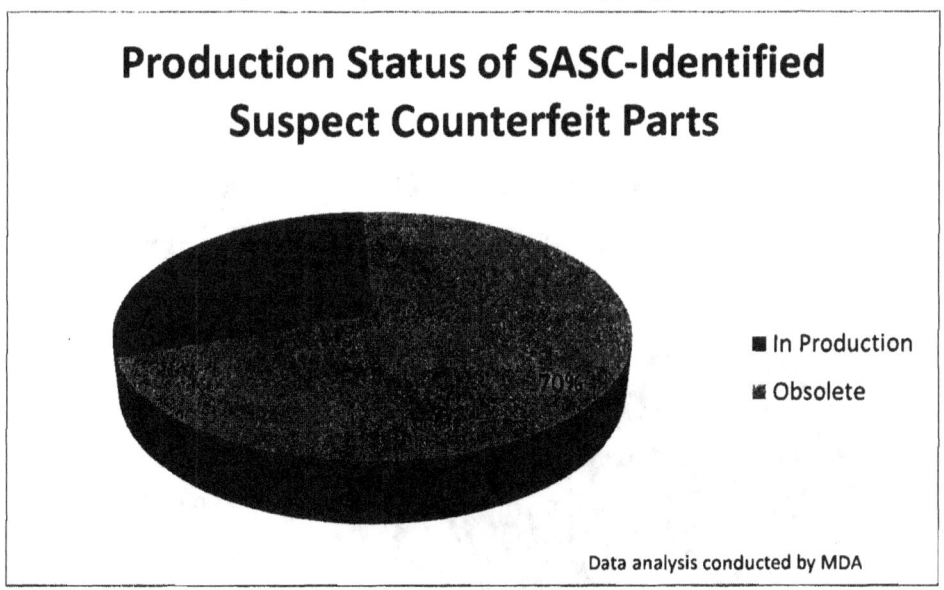

Data analysis conducted by MDA

Suppliers of the 1,800 parts were overwhelmingly independent distributors. MDA's finding that 30 percent of the 1,500 suspect parts that they were able to track were still in production indicates that companies in the defense supply chain are using independent distributors as a source for parts that may be available from manufacturers or authorized distributors. That is despite the risk of acquiring a counterfeit part being far higher when purchasing from an independent distributor than from a manufacturer or a manufacturer's authorized distributor.

In addition to determining whether parts were obsolete or in production, MDA also compared the lot date codes of parts in the SASC-supplied list to the original component manufacturer's end of production (EOP) date, i.e., the date on which the manufacturer has indicated that production of the part would end. MDA found 114 cases where the date listed on a part from the SASC list postdated the manufacturer's EOP date; in other words, 114 parts were dated after production of those parts had apparently already ceased. That finding highlights the importance of prospective buyers comparing date codes on a part's package to manufacturer EOP dates.

2. Performance Grade of Suspect Counterfeit Parts

MDA was able to identify the performance grade of approximately 60 percent of the part numbers provided by the Committee. As discussed above, a part's performance grade indicates the temperature range over which the part is expected to operate effectively. Electronic parts marked as military grade are designed to operate over a broader temperature range than those marked industrial or commercial grade and may be used when it is expected that a device may be exposed to extreme conditions.[72] As reflected in Figure 5, MDA found that 20 percent of the

---

[72] McCloskey Sentencing Memorandum at 7.

suspect parts on the SASC-provided list were military grade and 50 percent were industrial grade, with the remaining 30 percent being commercial grade or lower.

Figure 4

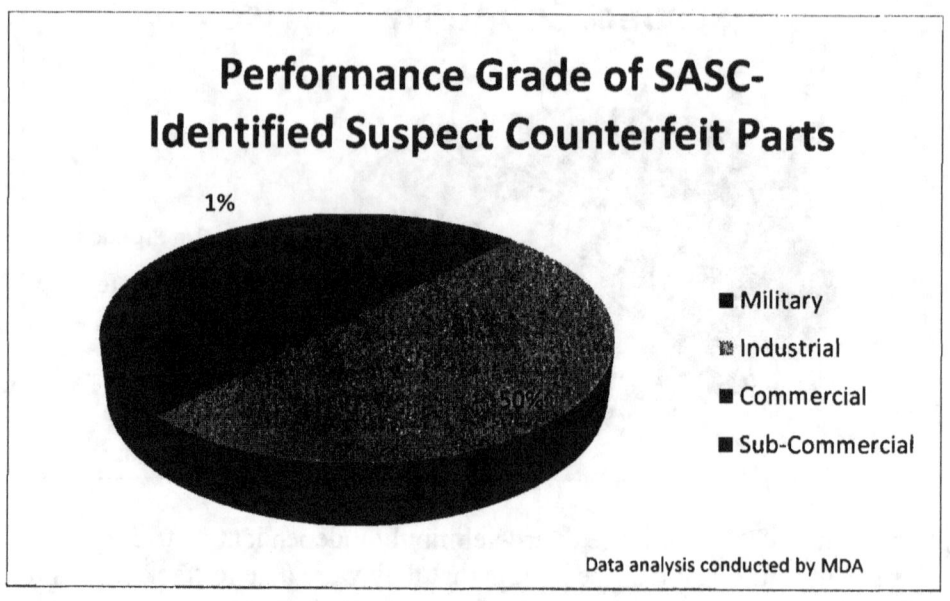

Some parts MDA identified as having military grade markings were suspect counterfeit because the labs that tested them found evidence that the original part numbers and other markings had been removed and the parts had been remarked. That finding raises the possibility that the parts may be commercial or industrial grade parts remarked as military grade. Remarking a commercial or industrial grade variant of a part as military grade poses a particular risk as such parts may pass basic testing but fail in the field when exposed to extreme conditions. Marking a part as higher grade is attractive to counterfeiters as such parts are likely to command a higher price. [73]

C. Reporting of SASC-Identified Suspect Counterfeit Parts

The Government-Industry Data Exchange Program (GIDEP) is a Department of Defense (DOD) program designated by the Office of Management and Budget (OMB) as "the government's central database for receiving and disseminating information about nonconforming products and materials."[74] GIDEP serves as a forum where government and industry participants can exchange information about material nonconformance, product end of life, and other issues. The program's purpose is to "reduce or eliminate unnecessary resource expenditures by sharing existing information between government and industry."[75]

---

[73] *Ibid.* at 12-13.

[74] GIDEP Fact Sheet, *available at* http://www.gidep.org/about/fact_sheets/fact_sheets.pdf#page=7 (last visited February 13, 2012).

[75] GIDEP Website, *available at* https://members.gidep.org/info/aboutus.htm (last visited February 13, 2012).

One category of information shared through GIDEP is Failure Experience Data (FED). Reports of suspect counterfeit electronic parts are submitted to GIDEP as FED reports.[76] FED reports involving suspect counterfeit parts include information such as a part's manufacturer, the part number, and a description of characteristics that led to it being deemed suspect. Reports may also indicate who supplied the part and include test reports and other data. GIDEP members can review reports online through the program's website.

Raytheon's Vice-President for Supply Chain Operations testified to the Committee that sharing information through GIDEP "can help stop suppliers of counterfeit parts in their tracks."[77] The effectiveness of GIDEP in serving that purpose, however, depends on whether members actually file reports in the system. The Committee found that reporting to be severely lacking.

While the Committee identified approximately 1,800 cases of suspect counterfeit parts in the defense supply chain in 2009 and 2010, only 271 total reports of suspect counterfeit parts were submitted to GIDEP during that period. Figure 6 shows the categories of filers. While OMB requires U.S. government agencies to participate in the FED portion of GIDEP (which includes counterfeit parts), agencies have apparently not interpreted "participation" to include filing reports of suspect counterfeit parts in the system. For example, while there were hundreds of cases between 2009 and 2010 in which DOD became aware of suspect counterfeit parts supplied to the military, only 13 GIDEP reports were filed by a government agency during that period.[78]

Figure 6

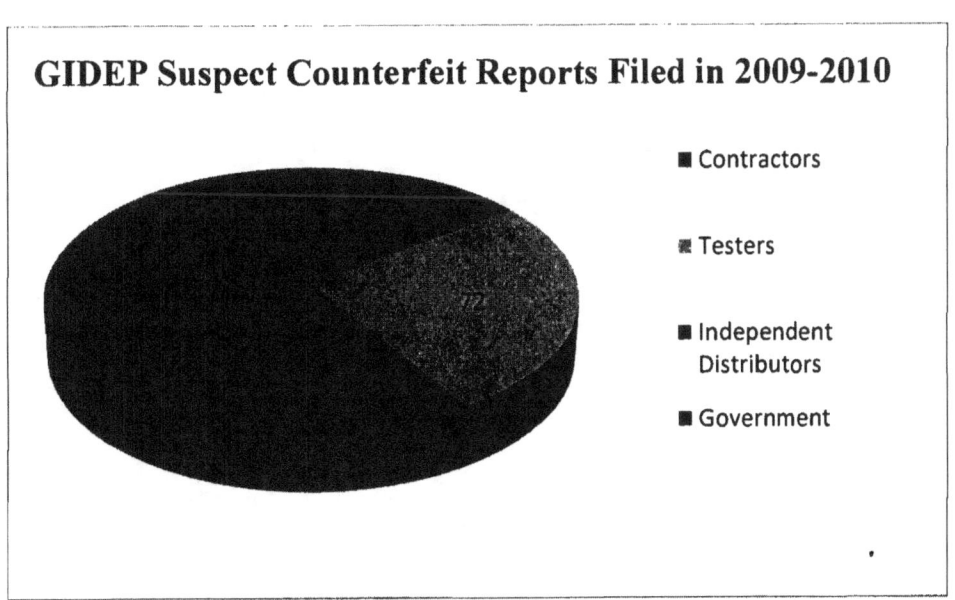

GIDEP Suspect Counterfeit Reports Filed in 2009-2010

- Contractors
- Testers
- Independent Distributors
- Government

---

[76] GIDEP Data, *available at* http://www.gidep.org/data/cft/cft.htm (last visited February 13, 2012).

[77] SASC Hearing at 84.

[78] Office of Management and Budget, *Policy Letter 91-3: Reporting Nonconforming Products* (April 9, 1991); Committee Staff GIDEP Database Search conducted in January 2012. DLA alone identified hundreds of cases of suspect counterfeit parts in 2009 and 2010. DLA, *Final Suspect Counterfeit Data for SASC* (March 28, 2011).

Several defense contractors and independent distributors told the Committee that they are reluctant to submit reports of suspect counterfeit electronic parts to GIDEP due to concerns about legal liability associated with GIDEP's requirement that they name the supplier of a suspect part. In an effort to address those concerns and increase reporting into the system, GIDEP issued an interim policy that allowed reports to be submitted without listing the supplier of the suspect counterfeit part.[79] That policy was instituted September 15, 2010 and expired on December 15, 2010.

While reporting increased significantly during the period in which the interim policy was in effect, with 187 reports submitted, 180 of those 187 reports were submitted by just six companies. In fact, a single company was responsible for more than half the total number of GIDEP reports filed during that period. Only five GIDEP reports were filed by defense contractors while the interim policy was in effect.[80]

On December 14, 2011, DOD issued a Department of Defense Instruction (DODI) stating that "all occurrences of suspect and confirmed counterfeit items will be documented in the appropriate reporting system to include the GIDEP."[81] The DODI also directed DOD's Director of Defense Procurement and Acquisition Policy to "develop procurement instructions and procedures . . . including appropriate contract language and reporting requirements to GIDEP and law enforcement agencies."[82]

---

[79] Memorandum from Jim Stein, GIDEP Program Manager, to GIDEP Members, *GIDEP Interim Policy Change Regarding "Reporting Suspect Counterfeit Parts and Materials"* (September 15, 2010) at 1.
[80] Committee Staff GIDEP Database Search Conducted in January 2012.
[81] Department of Defense, *Instruction 4140.01: DOD Supply Chain Materiel Management Policy* (December 14, 2011) at 13.
[82] *Ibid.* at 8.

III.   GAO Investigation into Online Sales of Counterfeit Parts

Advances in the technology and processes used by counterfeiters have made it increasingly difficult to detect counterfeit electronic parts. At the same time, the Internet has given counterfeiters access to a worldwide market for their goods. In fact, USTR reports that growth in the online sale of all counterfeits, not just electronic parts, "is rapidly approaching the volume of goods that [are] sold by street vendors and in other physical markets."[83]

With respect to internet purchases of electronic parts, customers can buy parts either directly from authorized or independent distributors or through Internet trading platforms. Such trading platforms include Broker Forum,[84] IC Source,[85] and netCOMPONENTS.[86]

The Committee sought to determine whether Internet-based trading platforms are being used to sell counterfeit electronic parts, and if so, where the suppliers of those counterfeit parts were located. The Committee requested that the Government Accountability Office's (GAO) Forensic Audit and Investigative Service (FAIS) purchase electronic parts through major online electronic parts trading platforms.[87] GAO's full report, *Suspect Counterfeit Electronic Parts Can Be Found on Internet Purchasing Platforms*, is attached as Appendix A to this report. The FAIS unit conducts GAO's forensic audits and investigative work.[88]

The Committee requested that GAO purchase electronic parts in each of the following three categories:

(1) Authentic electronic parts that may be used in a military application but are obsolete and difficult to find;

(2) Electronic parts that may be used in a military application, have a part number that is authentic, but a date code that is beyond the date on which production of the parts ended; and

(3) Electronic parts that have a part number not associated with an authentic part.[89]

The three categories were selected to determine not only whether counterfeit electronic parts that are used in military applications are available on the trading platforms, but also the extent to which counterfeiters were willing to create counterfeit parts with fake part numbers.

---

[83] United States Trade Representative, *2011 Special 301 Report* (April 2011) at 10.

[84] Broker Forum describes itself as "[t]he world's largest online network for buyers and vendors of electronic components." Broker Forum Website, *available at* http://www.brokerforum.com (last visited January 11, 2011).

[85] IC Source describes itself as a "global leader among information clearinghouses for the electronic components brokering industry." IC Source Website, *available at* http://www.icsource.com (last visited January 11, 2011).

[86] netCOMPONENTS describes itself as "[t]he world's largest destination for the sourcing and procurement of electronic components in a direct, disclosed (non-anonymous) and vendor-neutral environment." netCOMPONENTS Website, *available at* http://www.netcomponents.com (last visited January 11, 2011).

[87] Letter from Senators Carl Levin and John McCain to The Honorable Gene Dodaro (August 2, 2011).

[88] GAO Presentation at National State Auditors Association Annual Conference, *GAO's Forensic Audits and Investigative Service Team: Tools and Methods to Identify Fraud, Waste and Abuse* (June 15, 2011) at 2-4.

[89] Letter from Senators Carl Levin and John McCain to The Honorable Gene Dodaro (August 2, 2011).

A. How the Part Numbers Were Selected for GAO

To assist in selecting parts numbers for GAO to solicit, the Committee consulted Missile Defense Agency (MDA) Quality and Safety Organization's Parts and Materials Advisory Group personnel at the Naval Surface Warfare Center (NSWC) Crane. As discussed above, NSWC-Crane maintains lifecycle information on electronic parts used in defense systems.

With respect to parts in Categories 1 and 2 above, NSWC-Crane provided the Committee a list of authentic part numbers for parts that are used in defense systems but are no longer in production.[90] The Committee asked the Defense Logistics Agency (DLA) to supply a list of defense systems that use those parts and the most recent date on which DLA purchased the parts.

As to parts in Category 3, NSWC-Crane took part numbers associated with authentic parts used in military systems and altered them slightly. For example, NSWC-Crane took the part number "AD536AJD" which is a converter manufactured by Analog Devices, and added the suffix /883B at the end. The /883B suffix indicates that the part has been screened to military standard 883 and may, therefore, be used in certain military and aerospace applications. However, Analog Devices does not manufacture an /883B version of the AD536AJD part, so any part marked "AD536AJD/883B" would be counterfeit.

The Committee provided GAO with a subset of the part numbers identified by NSWC-Crane. For Categories 1 and 2, the Committee provided GAO with NSWC-Crane identified part numbers associated with electronic parts that are used in at least two defense systems and have been purchased by DLA in the previous 10 years.[91] For Category 2, i.e., parts with a date code beyond the date on which production of the parts ended, the Committee recommended that GAO use parts from Category 1 but with production dates that postdate the manufacturer's last time buy date by three years.

With respect to Category 3, i.e., electronic parts that have a part number not associated with any authentic part, the Committee provided GAO with a list of fake part numbers.[92] GAO confirmed that the fake part numbers were not associated with legitimate parts.[93]

B. GAO Shell Company Solicits Parts on Internet Trading Platforms

GAO created a fictitious company with a "fictitious owner and employees, mailing and e-mail addresses, a website, and a listing on the Central Contractor Registration."[94] GAO sought

---

[90] For each of those part numbers NSWC-Crane provided the Committee with the name of the manufacturer, the part number, the last-time-buy-date, the part's performance grade, a description of the part and its potential criticality to a military system. NSWC-Crane also provided the Committee Staff with the manufacturer's specification sheet for each part.

[91] GAO independently verified with DLA that the parts were used for military applications. GAO, GAO-12-375, *DOD Supply Chain: Suspect Counterfeit Electronic Parts Can Be Found on Internet Purchasing Platforms* (February 2012) at 2 (hereinafter "GAO Report").

[92] The Committee also provided GAO with information about the legitimate part from which the fake part number was derived and an explanation of how the fake part number varied from the legitimate part number.

[93] GAO Report at 2.

[94] *Ibid.*

membership for the fake company on three internet trading platforms. Two of the platforms granted membership to the fake company.[95]

Using the fake company, GAO posted requests for parts on the two trading platforms. GAO "requested parts from vendors that were new in original packaging, not refurbished, and had no mixed date codes."[96] To simulate the purchasing behavior of actual customers, GAO offered to purchase parts from "the first vendor among those offering the lowest prices that provided enough information, such as name, addresses, and payment method, to make a purchase."[97] GAO independently retained SMT Corporation to conduct authentication testing on the parts in Categories 1 and 2 that it purchased.[98]

C. GAO Results

GAO purchased 16 parts from 13 separate vendors. Each of those suppliers was located in China. In fact, of the 396 vendors that responded to GAO solicitations, 334 were located in China.[99] Thirteen of the parts that GAO received were shipped from Shenzhen, and the other three were shipped from Hong Kong.[100]

1. Category 1: Authentic, but Obsolete and Difficult to Find Parts

GAO purchased seven authentic, but obsolete and difficult to find parts that are used in military applications.[101] All of the parts were supplied by companies in China and all were found to be suspect counterfeit.[102]

The seven parts purchased under Category 1 are used in a large number of defense systems including the Air Force's F-15 Eagle fighter plane, the Maverick AGM-65A missile, the Navy's E-C2 Hawkeye aircraft, the Marine Corp's V-22 Osprey tiltrotor aircraft, and the Navy's SSN-688 Los Angeles Class nuclear-powered attack submarine.[103] One is a memory chip that has been used in "at least 41 different DOD weapons systems."[104]

All of the seven parts purchased under Category 1 failed SMT Corporation's "visual inspection" testing.[105] Visual inspection is performed to "look for legitimate nonconformance" issues, such as refurbished or re-plated leads, surface scratches or cracks, or inconsistent part markings.[106] Parts showed inconsistent part markings, refurbished leads and different color

---

[95] *Ibid.*

[96] *Ibid.*

[97] *Ibid.*

[98] *Ibid.* at 3.

[99] *Ibid.* Of the remaining 62 companies, 25 were located in the United States, and 37 in other countries. *Ibid.*

[100] *Ibid.* at 4.

[101] For three of the parts, GAO purchased duplicates of the same part from two different vendors. *Ibid.*

[102] *Ibid.* at highlights page, 6.

[103] *Ibid.* at 7-10.

[104] *Ibid.* at 9-10.

[105] *Ibid.* at 6.

[106] *Ibid.* at 17; SMT Corporation, *Component Inspection Analysis N. 00006484* (October 20, 2011) at 3.

epoxy seals or surfaces within the same lot, often with scuff marks from re-tooling.[107] One of the parts had a "deformed" version of the manufacturer's logo on top of the component.[108] Six out of seven of the parts also failed "delidding and die microscopy" where the internal die is exposed to determine its legitimacy.[109] Testing revealed that parts within the same lot had different die, a red flag for suspect counterfeit parts.[110]

2. Category 2: Parts with Authentic Part Numbers but with Invalid Date Codes

GAO purchased five parts with authentic part numbers but with date codes beyond the last production date of the part.[111] By definition, all of the parts were counterfeit as, at a minimum, they had been remarked. All of the parts purchased by GAO came from companies in China. Although the parts were counterfeit by virtue of the date code, GAO had the parts tested for other indicia of counterfeiting.

All of the parts purchased under Category 2 failed visual inspection.[112] Many of the parts exhibited scratch or scuff marks, different color epoxy seal or surfaces, and refurbished or substandard leads.[113] All five of the parts also failed "scanning electron microscopy (SEM) analysis" which allows the testers to perform a magnified exterior visual inspection.[114] SEM analysis revealed three parts with evidence of "lapping."[115] Lapping is a "process in which material is precisely removed from a specimen to produce a desired dimension, surface finish or shape."[116] The other two parts revealed surface scratches during the SEM analysis.[117]

---

[107] SMT Corporation, *Component Inspection Analysis N. 00006484* (October 20, 2011) at 2; SMT Corporation, *Component Inspection Analysis N. 00006483* (October 20, 2011) at 2; SMT Corporation, *Component Inspection Analysis N. 00006646* (November 3, 2011) at 2; SMT Corporation, *Component Inspection Analysis N. 00007160* (December 20, 2011) at 2; SMT Corporation, *Component Inspection Analysis N. 00007306* (December 27, 2011) at 2; SMT Corporation, *Component Inspection Analysis N. 00007220* (December 22, 2011) at 2.

[108] SMT Corporation, *Component Inspection Analysis N. 00006646* (November 3, 2011) at 2, 13.

[109] GAO Report at 6, 18.

[110] *Ibid.* at 18; SMT Corporation, *Component Inspection Analysis N. 00006484* (October 20, 2011) at 2; SMT Corporation, *Component Inspection Analysis N. 00006483* (October 20, 2011) at 2; SMT Corporation, *Component Inspection Analysis N. 00006646* (November 3, 2011) at 2; SMT Corporation, *Component Inspection Analysis N. 00007306* (December 27, 2011) at 2.

[111] GAO Report at 11.

[112] *Ibid.* at 12.

[113] SMT Corporation, *Component Inspection Analysis N. 00006485* (October 20, 2011) at 2; SMT Corporation, *Component Inspection Analysis N. 00006575* (October 27, 2011) at 2; SMT Corporation, *Component Inspection Analysis N. 00007103* (December 14, 2011) at 2; SMT Corporation, *Component Inspection Analysis N. 00007274* (December 20, 2011) at 2; SMT Corporation, *Component Inspection Analysis N. 00007242* (December 27, 2011) at 2.

[114] GAO Report at 12, 17.

[115] SMT Corporation, *Component Inspection Analysis N. 00006575* (October 27, 2011) at 2; SMT Corporation, *Component Inspection Analysis N. 00007103* (December 14, 2011) at 2; SMT Corporation, *Component Inspection Analysis N. 00007274* (December 20, 2011) at 2.

[116] SMT Corporation, *Component Inspection Analysis N. 00006575* (October 27, 2011) at 2.

[117] SMT Corporation, *Component Inspection Analysis N. 00006485* (October 20, 2011) at 2; SMT Corporation, *Component Inspection Analysis N. 00007242* (December 27, 2011) at 2.

3. Category 3: Parts with Bogus Part Numbers

GAO purchased four parts with bogus or made-up part numbers.[118] All of the parts came from companies in China. GAO did not submit these parts for testing since none of the part numbers are "associated with parts that have ever been manufactured."[119]

The results of GAO's operation reveal the ease with which counterfeiters are able to access customers and the extremes to which counterfeiters are willing to go to sell counterfeit products. The results also add to the already overwhelming evidence that China-based companies are the primary source of counterfeit electronic parts on the market.

---

[118] GAO Report at 15. GAO also solicited quotations for a "totally fictitious part number that was not based on an actual part number . . .." GAO received a quotation from a vendor willing to supply the completely fictitious part, but did not invest the resources to purchase it. *Ibid.* at 16.
[119] *Ibid.* at 15.

IV.   Case Studies of Suspect Counterfeit Parts Integrated into Defense Systems

To illustrate the risks posed by counterfeit electronic parts, the Committee investigated several cases where suspect parts were actually integrated into critical defense systems used by the U.S. Navy and U.S. Air Force.

A.   *Suspect Counterfeit Parts Intended for Use in Navy Helicopters*

The SH-60B Seahawk is a Navy helicopter that conducts surface warfare and undersea surface warfare, surveillance, medical evacuation, mine detection, pilot rescue, and targeting support.[120] The SH-60B deploys on Navy cruisers, destroyers, and frigates and has a Forward Looking InfraRed system (FLIR) which provides low light and night vision capability.[121] The FLIR system also contains a laser used for targeting the SH-60B's Hellfire missiles.[122] Raytheon Company is the prime contractor to the Navy for the FLIR system.[123]

On September 8, 2011, Raytheon notified the U.S. Naval Supply Systems Command that suspect counterfeit transistors had been integrated into three Electromagnetic Interference Filters (EIF) contained in Electronics Units delivered to the Navy and intended for use in FLIR systems.[124] According to the Navy, the EIF is "a device for suppressing conducted interference either from external sources (aircraft RADAR, ship RADAR, Communications Systems, etc.) or internal sources (FLIR components) so as to not adversely affect FLIR performance."[125] Each FLIR Electronics Unit contains a single EIF.[126]

While stating that the FLIR system is not "flight safety critical,"[127] the Navy has said the failure of an EIF could cause the FLIR system to fail.[128] Without a functioning FLIR, an SH-60B could not conduct surface warfare missions involving Hellfire missiles.[129] A FLIR failure would also compromise the pilot's ability to avoid hazards and identify targets at night, affecting the ability of SH-60Bs pilots to conduct night operations.[130] Raytheon was unaware of the suspect counterfeit parts in the EIFs until alerted to it by the Committee's investigation.[131]

---

[120] Letter from Mark Esper to Senators Carl Levin and John McCain (September 9, 2011); Email from Louise Vitale to Joe Bryan et al. (September 13, 2011).

[121] Letter from Mark Esper to Senators Carl Levin and John McCain (September 9, 2011).

[122] Email from Louise Vitale to Joe Bryan et al. (September 13, 2011).

[123] Committee Staff briefing with NAVAIR & NAVSUP, U.S. Navy (September 23, 2011).

[124] Letter from Daniel Forbes to Kathy Andrews (September 8, 2011).

[125] Email from Louise Vitale to Joe Bryan et al. (September 13, 2011).

[126] Email from CAPT Don Martin to Joe Bryan (September 30, 2011).

[127] The Navy defines "Flight Safety Critical Aircraft Part" as "a part, assembly, installation, or production system with one or more critical or critical safety characteristics that, if missing or not conforming to the design data, quality requirements, or overhaul and maintenance documentation, would result in an unsafe condition that could cause loss or serious damage to the end item or major components, loss of control, uncommanded engine shutdown, or serious injury or death to personnel." NAVAIR Instruction 4200.25D.

[128] Email from CAPT Don Martin to Joe Bryan (September 30, 2011).

[129] Committee Staff briefing with NAVAIR & NAVSUP, U.S. Navy (September 23, 2011).

[130] *Ibid.*

[131] Committee Staff interview of Vivek Kamath (October 6, 2011) at 59.

1. Electronic Parts Recycler Sells Transistors to EIF Manufacturer

The Committee identified the suspect transistors as it was tracking parts back through the supply chain to their original source. In response to a request from the Committee, Oneida Research Services (ORS), an electronic part testing laboratory, identified a number of suspect counterfeit parts it had identified, including suspect counterfeit transistors that it had tested for Global IC Trading Group (Global IC), an independent distributor.[132] The marking on the suspect transistors indicated that they were Fairchild Semiconductor devices.[133]

Oneida's testing, however, identified a number of anomalies with the devices. The test report stated that "[m]old markings on the top side of the package showed obvious differences in appearance and also appeared to be 'black-topped.'"[134] The lab found "non-uniform" leads as well as "deep scratches" on the parts and said, "[d]ie markings did not correspond to that of the external package markings."[135] It found "[d]amage around the mounting hole" that was possibly suggestive of previous mounting.[136] Oneida reported that the "leads may have been cut from solder joints, re-fitted by welds and solder coated."[137] Oneida concluded that "results of the analysis suggest the devices have possibly been refurbished components or possible counterfeits."[138]

Global IC informed the Committee that it had purchased the parts in July 2010 from a company called Technology Conservation Group (TCG), an electronic parts recycler and independent distributor.[139] Global IC had submitted the parts to Oneida for testing because its customer, L-3 Communications Display Systems, "requires product to be tested by Oneida prior to shipping."[140] According to Global IC, in addition to the two samples that failed Oneida's testing, 22 pieces failed Global IC Trading Group's own inspection.[141] Global IC returned the parts to TCG and did not ship any of the transistors to L-3 Display Systems.[142]

TCG, the Committee discovered, received the parts from a television broadcast company, Thomson Broadcast in Southwick, Massachusetts.[143] Thomson Broadcast told the Committee that it purchased the parts in 2008 but had decided to scrap them due to "date codes outside the

---

[132] Letter from Daniel J. Rossiter to United States Senate Committee on Armed Services (March 22, 2011).

[133] Oneida, *Counterfeit Screening Report N. 186947-001* (August 23, 2010).

[134] *Ibid.* at 2.

[135] *Ibid.* at 2-3.

[136] *Ibid.*

[137] *Ibid.*

[138] *Ibid.*

[139] Letter from Lori LeRoy to Ilona Cohen (June 24, 2011); Global IC, *Fairchild, RFG60P06E, DC 0548* (undated) (attached to June 24, 2011 letter).

[140] Letter from Lori LeRoy to Ilona Cohen (June 24, 2011); Global IC, *Fairchild, RFG60P06E, DC 0548* (undated) (attached to June 24, 2011 letter).

[141] Letter from Lori LeRoy to Ilona Cohen (June 24, 2011); Global IC, *Fairchild, RFG60P06E, DC 0548* (undated) (attached to June 24, 2011 letter).

[142] Letter from Lori LeRoy to Ilona Cohen (June 24, 2011); Global IC, *Fairchild, RFG60P06E, DC 0548* (undated) (attached to June 24, 2011 letter).

[143] Letter from Michele Lieberman to Chairman Levin and Committee Members (August 1, 2011).

usable range appropriate for resale."[144] According to TCG, the parts arrived from Thomson Broadcast in what they said appeared to be the original packaging so TCG labeled them as "new."[145]

According to TCG, after parts are sold by the company they undergo "additional quality control visual and scope inspection" before being shipped to the customer.[146] The Committee sought further information from TCG regarding the "quality control visual and scope inspection" performed on the suspect transistors, but was informed that the company no longer had "written documentation as to the specific tests or processes utilized to examine this part."[147]

In addition to Global IC, TCG also offered the parts to another company, Sigma Technology Inc., Ltd. An email from TCG to Sigma stated that "the parts have cosmetic issues" and included photos.[148] Sigma responded that the parts could not be approved and cancelled the order.[149] After both Global IC and Sigma rejected the parts, TCG decided that they had a "higher scrap value then [sic] resale value" and scrapped the remaining pieces in its inventory.[150] By that point, however, the company had already sold 60 transistors from that same lot to a third company, Texas Spectrum Electronics.[151] The Committee found no evidence that TCG ever informed Texas Spectrum that two other companies rejected the parts.

2. Texas Spectrum Uses Suspect Counterfeit Transistors from TCG in EIFs

Texas Spectrum incorporated the transistors it bought from TCG into Electromagnetic Interference Filters (EIF) and shipped eight of the filters to Raytheon in December 2010.[152] Between January and August 2011, Raytheon sold three of those eight EIFs to the U.S. Navy in FLIR electronics units and three to Fujitsu in support of the Japanese Ministry of Defense.[153] Two EIFs remain at Raytheon.[154]

The Navy used the three electronics units containing EIFs with suspect parts as spares sent to the U.S.S. Gridley in Sasebo, Japan; the Helicopter Anti-Sub Light Squad 60 in Mayport, Florida; and the U.S. Naval Station, also in Mayport.[155] The U.S. Gridley spent most of the time between March 2011, when Raytheon shipped the electronics unit containing the suspect counterfeit part, and September 2011, when the company alerted the U.S. Navy to the problem,

---

[144] While Thomson Broadcast had shipped the parts to TCG as "E-scrap," TCG had Thomson Broadcast's permission to sell the parts. Email from Henry Blake to Florence Robinson (March 3, 2010) ("Everything can be sold except material that is marked 'Thomson.'"); Emails from Henry Blake to Ozge Guzelsu (August 10, 2011).

[145] Letter from Michele Lieberman to Chairman Levin and Committee Members (September 19, 2011).

[146] Ibid.

[147] TCG further stated, "Any and all hand written notes are destroyed after (90) days, which is the period provided for returns." Ibid.

[148] Email from Karen Willis to Renna Wang et al. (August 21, 2010).

[149] Email from Renna Wang to Karen Willis (August 24, 2010).

[150] Letter from Michele Lieberman to Chairman Levin and Committee Members (August 1, 2011).

[151] Ibid.

[152] Letter from Mark Esper to Senators Carl Levin and John McCain, and attachments (August 23, 2011).

[153] Ibid. Raytheon sent notification of the suspect counterfeits in the filters intended for the Japanese Ministry of Defense on September 8, 2011. Letter from Jeff Derrick to Silas Reed (September 8, 2011).

[154] Letter from Mark Esper to Senators Carl Levin and John McCain (August 23, 2011).

[155] Letter from Mark Esper to Senators Carl Levin and John McCain (September 9, 2011).

deployed to the Western Pacific with the USS Carl Vinson carrier strike group, conducting surface surveillance and control missions.[156] The electronics unit shipped to the Naval Station in Mayport was installed on a helicopter that flew training missions and post-maintenance check flights before the unit was removed on September 23, 2011. The unit shipped to the Anti-Sub Light Squad 60 was never placed into service on an aircraft and remained in "ready for issue" status until it was replaced by Raytheon.[157]

3. Suspect Counterfeit Transistors Traced to China

The Committee asked Thomson Broadcast where it had purchased the suspect transistors it provided to TCG. Thomson Broadcast reported that it had bought the parts in April 2008 from a company in California called E-Warehouse.[158] E-Warehouse, in turn, purchased the parts in April 2008 from a UK-based company called Pivotal Electronics.[159] Pivotal bought them that same month from Huajie Electronics Ltd., a distributor in Shenzhen, China.[160]

As described above, Oneida Research Services, Global IC, and Sigma Technology all identified anomalies with the parts as they moved through the supply chain. However, they were not the first to identify anomalies. E-Warehouse's April 2008 purchase order for the parts indicated problems with their condition, including indicating "N" for "no" to the following questions:

"If pin indicator present is it formed properly and consistent? N"
"Are parts free of moisture, dirt, abrasive appearance and paint? N"
"Are part leads straight, and any coating consistent in appearance? N"
"Are parts free of oxidation, abrasive sand, or other foreign materials? N"
"Is certificate of traceability included with shipping documents? N"[161]

Nevertheless, E-Warehouse shipped the parts to Thomson Broadcast. E-Warehouse told the Committee that it informed Thomson at the time that the company "did not have the capability to electronically test the product prior to delivery without a substantial testing fee" and "an additional three week processing time."[162] According to E-Warehouse, Thomson Broadcast "was desperate for the parts and requested [E-Warehouse] proceed with the agreement. They would be responsible to test the product prior to installation on their products."[163]

---

[156] Email from CAPT Don Martin to Joe Bryan (September 30, 2011); Commander Naval Surface Force, U.S. Pacific Fleet, *Gridley Returns to San Diego After Successful Deployment*, available at http://www.public.navy.mil/surfor/ddg101/Pages/GridleyReturnstoSanDiegoAfterSuccessfulDeployment.aspx (last visited July 22, 2011).

[157] Email from Louise Vitale to Joe Bryan (February 22, 2012); Email from Louise Vitale to Joe Bryan (February 21, 2012).

[158] Email from Henry Blake to Ozge Guzelsu (August 10, 2011). E-Warehouse is also known as Xelon Corporation. Email from Walter Simpson to Ozge Guzelsu (August 30, 2011).

[159] Pivotal Electronics Proforma Invoice N. PS04040806 (April 4, 2008).

[160] Pivotal Electronics Purchase Order N. PIV11034 (April 4, 2008).

[161] Xelon Corporation Purchase Order Receiver N. 402728 (April 2, 2008).

[162] E-Warehouse Packing Slip N. 22867 (April 23, 2008); Email from Walter Simpson to Ozge Guzelsu (August 30, 2011).

[163] Email from Michael Coots to Ozge Guzelsu (September 2, 2011).

4. Raytheon Investigates Provenance of Suspect Parts

In August 2011, the Committee alerted Texas Spectrum that the transistors the company purchased from TCG were suspect counterfeit.[164] Texas Spectrum subsequently advised Raytheon that the parts were suspect. That notification led to Raytheon initiating its own investigation.[165]

Raytheon asked the purported manufacturer, Fairchild Semiconductor, about the parts.[166] A Fairchild engineer told Raytheon the parts were "suspicious" and said the surface of the parts "reminds me of previous cases of counterfeit parts that had the top package re-surfaced and re-marked."[167] The engineer concluded that "[b]ased on the available information, I would say that the origin of these parts are questionable."[168]

In October 2011, the Committee asked Fairchild Semiconductor about the authenticity of the transistors, given the anomalies that Oneida Research Services had identified when it tested the transistors.[169] Fairchild responded, "We believe these devices are not genuine Fairchild devices."[170]

5. Raytheon Informs the U.S. Navy of Suspect Counterfeit Parts

In September 2011, Raytheon notified the U.S. Navy that the company "had become aware of suspect counterfeit components" used in the EIFs intended for use in FLIRs on the SH-60B.[171] Raytheon did not, however, recommend recalling the electronics units containing the affected EIFs, stating:

> This notice is being provided for information only. Until this issue is resolved, or test data indicate otherwise, Raytheon is not recommending a forced replacement of these suspect counterfeit EMI Filters at this time.[172]

On September 27, 2011, the Navy responded to Raytheon, stating that it considered the EIFs containing the suspect counterfeit transistors "as non-conforming material under the contract" and requested that Raytheon replace the filters "at no additional cost to the Government."[173] On September 30, 2011, Raytheon agreed to replace the filters at the company's expense.[174] Raytheon shipped replacement units to the U.S. Navy in October and November 2011.[175]

---

[164] Letter from Senators Carl Levin and John McCain to Michael Coots (August 5, 2011).
[165] Letter from Daniel Forbes to Kathy Andrews (September 8, 2011). The letter states, "On August 15 2011, Raytheon was notified by TSE of the suspect counterfeit MOSFETs used in the EMI filters."
[166] Email from Raquel Supangan to Jeremy Bettge (August 22, 2011).
[167] *Ibid.*
[168] *Ibid.*
[169] Letter from Senators Carl Levin and John McCain to Mark Thompson (October 20, 2011).
[170] Letter from Paul Delva to Ozge Guzelsu and Bryan Parker (October 25, 2011).
[171] Letter from Daniel Forbes to Kathy Andrews (September 8, 2011).
[172] *Ibid.* (emphasis in original).
[173] Letter from Kathy Andrews to Daniel Forbes (September 27, 2011).
[174] Letter from Daniel Forbes to Kathy Andrews (September 30, 2011).
[175] Email from Chip Kennett to Ozge Guzelsu (February 17, 2012).

B. *Suspect Counterfeit Parts in C-27J Avionics Systems*

The C-27J is a U.S. Air Force airplane used for tactical transport and to support combat operations.[176] L-3 Integrated Systems, a division of L-3 Communications, is the prime contractor to the Air Force on the C-27J.[177] The Air Force has ordered 38 C-27Js from L-3, 12 of which have been delivered. As of February 2012, two C-27Js were deployed to Afghanistan.[178]

One avionics item on the C-27J is called a Bus Adaptor Unit or BAU. The Air Force likened the BAU to a "switchboard at an office" that allows different systems to talk to one another.[179] "The BAUs are primarily used to interface non-MIL-STD-1553B systems with the Avionics bus architecture system."[180] In particular, the BAU Type I communicates with the Mission Computer to monitor systems like the plane's de-icing systems and anti-skid controller and provide lighting for avionics cockpit panels.[181]

On September 19, 2011, L-3 informed the Air Force that Alenia Aeronautica, a subcontractor to L-3 Integrated Systems, had notified it "of the inclusion of suspect electronic components in several avionics items within the Joint Cargo Aircraft C-27J hardware previously delivered to the Government."[182] In August 2009, almost two years prior to L-3's notification, the Goodrich Company had notified Alenia that suspect counterfeit electronic parts had been integrated into circuit cards sold to Goodrich by its circuit card supplier, Raven Industries.[183] Goodrich had integrated the affected circuit cards in Bus Adapter Type 1 Units (BAU) that it sold to Alenia.[184]

Alenia, however, not only failed in 2009 to notify its prime contractor, L-3 Integrated Systems, but it also failed to remove the affected BAUs. It was not until Alenia received an inquiry from the Committee in August 2011 that the company notified L-3 of the suspect counterfeit parts and L-3 notified the U.S Air Force.[185]

1. Supplier Buys Parts from China

On October 14, 2008, Raven Industries, a subcontractor to the Goodrich Company, issued a purchase order to New Advantage, an independent electronic parts distributor in St. Petersburg,

---

[176] Alenia Aeronautica Website, *available at* http://www.aleniana.com/c-27j-spartan-tactical-transport-aircraft (last visited April 16, 2012).

[177] L-3 Communications, *Press Release: L-3 Communications Integrated Systems Announces C-27 JCA Final Proposal Submittal* (February 2, 2007).

[178] Email from Lt Col James DeLong to Ozge Guzelsu (February 17, 2012).

[179] Committee Staff briefing with U.S. Air Force (September 30, 2011).

[180] Alenia Aeronautica, *Additional Response to the Senate Armed Services Committee Request for BAU Type I Safety Evaluation* (September 13, 2011).

[181] Alenia Aeronautica, *Additional Response to the Senate Armed Services Committee Request for BAU Type I Safety Evaluation* (September 13, 2011).

[182] Letter from L-3 Communications Integrated Systems to the Department of the Air Force (September 19, 2011).

[183] Letter from John Dattilio to Frederico Piccotti (August 17, 2009) at 1.

[184] *Ibid.*

[185] Committee Staff interview of Luca Napolitano (October 5, 2011) at 20; Letter from Senators Carl Levin and John McCain to John Young (August 31, 2011).

Florida, and one of Goodrich's approved vendors, for 10,000 metal–oxide–semiconductor field-effect transistors (MOSFET).[186] Raven intended to use the MOSFETs to build circuit cards for Goodrich.[187] In January 2009, New Advantage purchased 2,000 MOSFETs from Green Globe Industry Company in Shenzhen, China.[188]

According to New Advantage policies in effect at the time, all electronic components purchased by the company from Asia were required to be tested at a third party testing firm "to a minimum of full functionality."[189] Consistent with that policy, New Advantage sent the MOSFETs it bought for Raven to White Horse Strategic Solutions, Ltd. in Shenzhen China, for testing. The order for testing stated that "[p]arts [are] to be tested to *ensure functionality*."[190]

On January 16, 2009, White Horse completed its test report concluding that "[a]ll tested parts passed at tested parameters."[191] New Advantage subsequently sent the MOSFETs to Raven in the first quarter of 2009. Raven used the parts to build a total of 242 circuit cards which it shipped to Goodrich in the first quarter of 2009.[192] Goodrich integrated a number of the circuit cards into BAUs intended for Alenia and other customers.[193]

2. Second Lot of Parts from China Identified as "Counterfeit Product"

In February 2009, New Advantage purchased a second lot of 1,600 MOSFET transistors from Green Globe.[194] Rather than having the parts tested in China, the company instead had them shipped to the United States.[195] New Advantage sent the parts for testing to Anloy Technologies, an independent test lab in Texas.[196]

Later that month, testing conducted by Anloy concluded that the transistors from Green Globe were "counterfeit product."[197] While the MOSFETs passed electrical testing, the test report noted that there were three different types of die in the four transistors that were examined and that product markings on the parts actually wiped off.[198] Additionally, the test report noted that some of the leads on the parts were "rough looking" while others were new.[199]

---

[186] Raven Industries Purchase Order N. 539076 to New Advantage (October 14, 2008).

[187] Letter from John Dattilio to Frederico Piccotti (August 17, 2009) at 1.

[188] New Advantage Purchase Order No. 264432 to Green Globe Industry Company (January 12, 2009).

[189] New Advantage, Asia *Procurement Policy* (rev. December 20, 2007). According to New Advantage, the company tested the parts in China to speed up the process and to avoid the large freight cost of shipping the parts to the United States. Email from LJ Hartnett to Ozge Guzelsu (September 21, 2011).

[190] New Advantage Purchase Order N. 264450 to White Horse (January 13, 2009) (emphasis added).

[191] White Horse, *Electrical Test Report Work Order N. SZO3339* (January 16, 2009) at 1.

[192] Letter from John Dattilio to Frederico Piccotti (August 17, 2009) at 1.

[193] Goodrich answers to August 9, 2011 written questions from Senators Carl Levin and John McCain (August 23, 2011). Goodrich also integrated the circuit cards into sub-systems for Boeing, Airbus, and Lockheed Martin. *Ibid.*

[194] Letter from Daniel Rykhus to Senators Carl Levin and John McCain (August 17, 2011) at 2; Green Globe Purchase Order N. 265898 to New Advantage (February 10, 2009).

[195] New Advantage said it "felt confident enough to have the order sent from Green Global directly to us . . . and test in the U.S.A. per our Asian Procurement Policy." Email from LJ Hartnett to Ozge Guzelsu (September 21, 2011).

[196] Email from LJ Hartnett to Ozge Guzelsu (September 21, 2011).

[197] Anloy Technologies, *Product Analysis Report N. ATI1625* (February 19, 2009) at 3.

[198] *Ibid.* at 1.

[199] *Ibid.*

On February 25, 2009, New Advantage informed Raven that the second lot of parts purchased from Green Globe had failed testing and that the company would be unable to fulfill the remainder of Raven's order for 10,000 parts.[200] New Advantage did not realize at that time that the 2,000 MOSFETs it had previously sold Raven shared the same lot code as the 1,600 MOSFETs identified by Anloy as suspect counterfeit.[201] As a result, New Advantage did not alert Raven that the previously supplied parts should also be considered suspect counterfeit.

3. Goodrich Discovers a Problem with the BAUs

On May 18, 2009, Goodrich identified multiple failures with MOSFETs used on circuit boards provided by Raven.[202] In investigating the cause of those failures, Raven discovered that the MOSFETs that were failing at Goodrich had not only been purchased from the same supplier, New Advantage, but also shared a date code with the MOSFETs that had been rejected as counterfeit product.[203]

On July 23, 2009, Raven alerted Goodrich that the circuit cards it had shipped to the company contained suspect counterfeit parts.[204] On August 17, 2009, Goodrich notified Alenia that two BAUs it had supplied the company contained suspect parts.[205] A week later, Goodrich sent a second letter to Alenia notifying the company that a total of five affected BAUs had been shipped to Alenia.[206]

4. Alenia Fails to Remove the Affected BAUs

An Alenia employee received the two letters from Goodrich and emailed them to the individual responsible at Alenia for quality control of the C-27J.[207] The second letter was attached to an email stating that Goodrich was recalling a total five BAUs that had been delivered to the company.[208] On August 26, 2009, the Alenia quality control official forwarded the two letters to other Alenia employees with an email that said, "I am forwarding the notification that Goodrich sent to indicate some of the 'BUS ADAPTER UNIT' are suspected of having defects and to recommend their warranty return for inspection and repair."[209] Among the recipients of the email was the person in charge of the division responsible for issuing a work instruction to remove the BAUs.[210]

---

[200] Letter from Daniel Rykhus to Senators Carl Levin and John McCain (August 17, 2011) at 2.
[201] Letter from John Dattilio to Frederico Piccotti (August 17, 2009) at 1.
[202] Email from John Dattilio to Tony Meyers et al. (May 18, 2009).
[203] Letter from Daniel Rykhus to Senators Carl Levin and John McCain (August 17, 2011) at 2.
[204] Goodrich, *Mosfet N-Channel 043113-1, dc 9727 Counterfeit Parts* (July 27, 2009).
[205] Letter from John Dattilio to Frederico Piccotti (August 17, 2009) at 1.
[206] Letter from John Dattilio to Frederico Piccotti (August 25, 2009) at at 3.
[207] Committee Staff interview of Luca Napolitano (October 5, 2011) at 12-14.
[208] Email from Frederico Bruno Piccotti to Ezio Bottini (August 26, 2009) (English courtesy translation from the Italian).
[209] Email from Ezio Bottini to Roberto Stefani et al. (August 26, 2009) (English courtesy translation from the Italian).
[210] *Ibid.*; Committee Staff interview of Luca Napolitano (October 5, 2011) at 22.

Despite follow-up emails from Alenia employees discussing the need to recall the BAUs, the units were not removed and replaced.[211] In fact, over the next sixteen months, Alenia delivered three C-27Js with affected BAUs to L-3 Integrated Systems in January, November and December of 2010.[212] Asked later about Alenia's failure to remove the BAUs, Luca Napolitano, the company's Program Manager for the C-27 JCA Program, admitted that Alenia had "mismanage[d]" the process.[213]

5. Alenia Notifies L-3 About Suspect Counterfeit Parts – L-3 Notifies Air Force

On September 19, 2011, more than two years after being notified about the suspect parts, Alenia sent L-3 Integrated Systems a letter stating:

> The aim of this correspondence is to inform L-3 that Alenia North America has been inquired by the Senate Armed Services Committee on suspect counterfeit parts in the Department of Defence's (DOD) supply chain relating to the C-27J Aircraft.[214]

The letter went on to advise L-3 Integrated Systems that BAUs containing suspect parts had been installed on 3 planes sold to the U.S. Air Force.[215] It noted that Alenia had been notified of the suspect counterfeits on August 17, 2009 and again on August 25, 2009.[216] The letter also stated:

> Following these notifications from our supplier Goodrich, instructions were given within Alenia to locate [BAUs containing the suspect counterfeit parts], and to return them to the supplier. These parts were not retrieved prior to the delivery of the C27J aircraft to the Customer(s). No notification has been provided to the Prime Contractor nor, to the best of our knowledge, to the DOD directly.[217]

Notwithstanding the letter's claim that instructions were given to locate the BAUs and return them to the supplier, Alenia's Program Manager for the C-27 JCA Program said that the "instructions" referenced were simply the internal Alenia emails forwarding the notification from Goodrich.[218]

On September 19, 2011, the same day it received the notification letter from Alenia, L-3 Integrated Systems notified the U.S. Air Force that "suspect electronic components" had been delivered to the government in BAUs.[219] L-3's letter stated that "the affected BAUs can be recalled for rework/replacement/repair at the Government's convenience."[220] On September 20, 2011, Alenia released a C-27J Service Bulletin mandating the removal and replacement of BAUs

---

[211] *See, e.g.*, email from Roberto Stefani to Ezio Bottino (August 26, 2009); Committee Staff interview of Luca Napolitano (October 5, 2011) at 20-22.

[212] Alenia Aeronautica, *Delivery Dates to AF on Planes with Parts S/N 1601, 1602, and 1570* (September 16, 2011).

[213] Committee Staff interview of Luca Napolitano (October 5, 2011) at 19-20.

[214] Letter from Agne Gudeleviciute to Rudy Elizondo (September 19, 2011).

[215] *Ibid.*

[216] *Ibid.*

[217] *Ibid.*

[218] Committee Staff interview of Luca Napolitano (October 5, 2011) at 34.

[219] Letter from Kimberly Kachura to James Leighty (September 19, 2011).

[220] *Ibid.*

containing suspect counterfeit components.[221] The three affected BAUs were finally replaced in November 2011, December 2011, and January 2012, respectively.[222]

C. Suspect Counterfeit Parts in the U.S. Air Force C-130J and C-27J

The C-130J and C-27J are military cargo planes equipped with display units that provide the pilot with information on the health of the airplane, including engine status, fuel use, location, and warning messages.[223] The display units are manufactured by L-3 Display Systems, a division of L-3 Communications. For the C-130J, L-3 Display Systems manufactures the display units for Lockheed Martin, the military's prime contractor for the C-130J. For the C-27J, L-3 Display Systems manufactures the display units for Alenia Aeronautica, a subcontractor to L-3 Integrated Systems, which is a separate division of L-3 Communications and the military's prime contractor for the C-27J.[224]

In November 2010, L-3 Display Systems detected that the company's in-house failure rate for a chip installed on display units had more than tripled, from 8.5% to 27%.[225] L-3 Display Systems also noticed that the same part had previously failed on a fielded military airplane.[226] The company sent the chip that failed on the fielded aircraft and other samples from the same lot for testing.[227] That testing identified "multiple abnormalities" with the chips, including a blacktopped surface. The tester concluded the parts were "suspect counterfeit."[228] Unfortunately, L-3 Display Systems had already installed parts from the suspect lot on more than 400 of its display units, including those intended for the C-27J, as well as the Air Force's C-130J.[229] Failure of the memory chip could cause a display unit to show a degraded image, lose data, or even go blank altogether.[230]

---

[221] Alenia Aeronautica, *C-27J Service Bulletin: Bus Adapter Unit (BAU) Type 1 Suspect Components* (September 16, 2011). The bulletin was not released until September 20, 2011, even though it is dated September 16, 2011. *See* Committee Staff interview of J. Gregory Bruich (October 11, 2011) at 47.

[222] Alenia Aeronautica answers to February 16, 2012 Committee Staff written questions (February 20, 2012).

[223] In the C-130J, the suspect counterfeit chips affected display units known as Color Multipurpose Display Units (CMDUs) and Multi-Functional Control Displays (MFCDs). In the C-27J, the suspect counterfeit chips affected only CMDUs, as the C-27J is not equipped with MFCDs. U.S. Air Force C-27J Program Office, *Response to SASC Questions* (October 6, 2011); U. S. Air Force C-130J Program Office, *Parts Description Matrix* (October 6, 2011).

[224] L-3 Display Systems Fact Sheet, *available at* http://www2.l-3com.com/displays/pdfs/fs_cockpits%20(low%20res).pdf (last accessed April 18, 2012); Committee Staff Interview of Luca Napolitano (October 5, 2011) at 3-12.

[225] L-3 Display Systems, *Notification to Lockheed Martin* (November 2010), attached to email from Chris Durre to David Stathem and Cynthia Zeigler (November 11, 2010); Email from Leigh Ream to Fern Hoinowski (November 30, 2010).

[226] According to an attorney for L-3 Communications, the unit that failed was returned by Lockheed Martin to L-3 Display Systems on June 21, 2010. Email from Jack Deschauer to Ilona Cohen et al. (November 5, 2011); L-3 Display Systems, *Notification to Lockheed Martin* (November 2010), attached to email from Chris Durre to David Stathem and Cynthia Zeigler (November 11, 2010).

[227] L-3 Display Systems, *Notification to Lockheed Martin* (November 2010), attached to email from Chris Durre to David Stathem and Cynthia Zeigler (November 11, 2010); SMT Corporation, *Component Inspection Analysis 00003485* (November 9, 2010).

[228] SMT Corporation, *Component Inspection Analysis 00003485* (November 9, 2010).

[229] The suspect counterfeit chip also went into a C-17 and a CH-46, a helicopter used by the Marine Corps for assault support. L-3 Display Systems, *Notification to Lockheed Martin* (November 2010), attached to email from Chris Durre to David Stathem and Cynthia Zeigler (November 11, 2010); L-3 Display Systems, *Notification to*

1. L-3 Display Systems' Detection of the Fake Memory Chip

In November 2010, approximately five months after a Video Random Access Memory (VRAM) chip had been returned for failure on a fielded C-130J, L-3 Display Systems detected a substantial increase in the failure rate of the same chip during their in-house testing.[231] L-3 Display Systems sent the memory chip that had failed on the fielded aircraft, as well as samples of the same chip that it had in stock, for "counterfeit part analysis" to SMT Corporation, a laboratory that specializes in testing of electronic parts.[232] SMT's testing identified "multiple abnormalities" with the chips. The company's test report found "variations in color and texture . . . along the package edges," stated that "the bottom surface of one sample exhibits markings when the other two samples do not," and found that "testing these components for marking permanency with acetone lifted a large amount of black material, revealing fine scratches in the original surface and confirming these parts are blacktopped."[233] The tester concluded that the parts were "not considered to be factory original parts" and were "suspect counterfeit."[234]

In November and December 2010, L-3 Display Systems sent its customers who had purchased affected display units notification letters, stating that the chip had been "tampered with, indicating that the components are suspect."[235] L-3 Display Systems advised its customers that there had been 141 internal failure occurrences (or 27%) and one field failure as a result of the chip.[236] L-3 Display Systems also reported that "the failure modes that may be exhibited by the displays" from the memory chip included "degraded visual imagery on the display," "blank screen/loss of display," and loss of data.[237]

On November 4, 2010, L-3 Display Systems issued a part purge notification, quarantining the company's own stock of the suspect counterfeit memory chip.[238] L-3 Display Systems did not, however, recommend to its customers that assemblies affected by the suspect counterfeit chips be returned for replacement of those chips.[239] As a result, hundreds of display

---

Alenia Aeronautica (December 16, 2010); L-3 Display Systems, *Notification to Boeing Corporation* (December 3, 2010); L-3 Display Systems, *Notification to Naval Air Systems Command* (December 3, 2010).

[230] According to L3, failure modes are mitigated by redundancy of multiple, configurable displays in the aircraft. L-3 Display Systems, *Notification to Lockheed Martin* at 2 (November 2010), attached to email from Chris Durre to David Stathem and Cynthia Zeigler (November 11, 2010).

[231] *Ibid.*

[232] SMT Corporation, *Component Inspection Analysis 00003485 and 00003485A* (November 9, 2010).

[233] *Ibid.*

[234] *Ibid.*

[235] *See, e.g.,* L-3 Display Systems, Notification to Lockheed Martin (November 2010), attached to email from Chris Durre to David Stathem and Cynthia Zeigler (November 11, 2010).

[236] *See, e.g., ibid.*

[237] *See, e.g., ibid.*

[238] L-3 Communications, *Part Purge Notification*, Control Number 2010-0069 (November 4, 2010).

[239] By contrast, in October 2009, nearly a year before the suspect Samsung part was discovered, L-3 Displays identified another counterfeit part – manufactured by Lattice – affecting its display units. The Lattice counterfeit part had been purchased by L-3 Display Systems from the same distributor, Global IC, and was supplied to Global IC by the same company in China, Hong Dark Electronic Trade. At the time, L-3 Displays notified its affected customers and stated that the failure modes that may be exhibited by the displays included "video anomalies in the display," and "blank screen." L-3 Display Systems described such a failure as a "potential safety" concern and offered to coordinate "replacement of any components." Those parts were removed, at L-3 Display Systems' expense, shortly after L-3 Display Systems' discovery and notification of the suspect counterfeit chip. Letter from

units intended for and installed on C-130Js and C-27Js included the suspect counterfeit memory chip, well after its discovery by L-3 Display Systems.

2. Suspect Counterfeit Memory Chip in the C-130J

In November 2010, when it notified Lockheed Martin, the Air Force's prime contractor on the C-130J, of the counterfeit memory chip, L-3 Display Systems identified more than 400 assemblies affected by the suspect counterfeit memory chip.[240]

a. Decision by Lockheed Martin to Take "No Action" on the Suspect Counterfeit Parts in the C-130J

When they received L-3 Display's formal notification, Lockheed Martin engineers discussed the suspect counterfeit parts internally. They decided that "no action" was necessary and the display units did not need to be returned for repair.[241] The Lead Engineer for C-130 Safety Programs at Lockheed Martin, Robert Giudice, concluded that the "condition in question appears to be that the LRU [line replaceable unit] may have a lower reliability than predicted," but noted that Lockheed Martin continued to meet its "safety objectives."[242] Giudice advised: There is "no short term increase in risk," and "nothing to be done from an operational perspective," but stated that "the solution to the issue is quite long-term."[243] The Chief Engineer for the C-130, who had ultimate responsibility at Lockheed for the decision to keep the suspect parts in the C-130s, accepted that advice and apparently put stock in the fact that the parts had passed ESS, or environmental stress screening, which he referred to as a "kind of a 'screening' of the counterfeit parts."[244]

The perception that a contractor's acceptance testing process or environmental stress screening – where systems containing the parts may be subjected to heat, vibration and other stresses – will weed out counterfeit parts was not limited to engineers at Lockheed Martin. In his interview with Committee staff, the President of L-3 Display Systems, Bruce Coffey, stated, "[T]here's a belief that our in-factory ESS profile, environmental stress screening, that we've performed is successful in screening out bad parts."[245]

However, according to General Patrick O'Reilly, the Director of the Missile Defense Agency (MDA), production testing is not sufficient to screen out all counterfeits. According to General O'Reilly:

A counterfeit part may pass all production testing. However, it is possible that the part was damaged during unauthorized processing (e.g., removing the part from a previous assembly, or sanding the surface in order to place a new part number)

Deborah K. Henning to Francesco Bucci (February 2, 2010); Committee Staff interview of J. Gregory Bruich (October 11, 2011) at 39.

[240] L-3 Display Systems, Notification to Lockheed Martin (November 2010), attached to email from Chris Durre to David Stathem and Cynthia Zeigler (November 11, 2010).

[241] Email from Brian Washington to Brian McKnight (November 12, 2010).

[242] Email from Robert Guidice to Stephen Horvath et al. (November 11, 2010).

[243] *Ibid.*

[244] Email from Stephen Horvath to Robert Guidice (November 11, 2010).

[245] Committee Staff interview of Bruce Coffey (October 13, 2011) at 42.

causing the deployed system to fail. Similarly, reliability may be affected because a counterfeit part may be near the end of its useful life when it is installed.[246]

The Committee asked Samsung Semiconductor, the manufacturer of the memory chip, about the reliability of a part that had the abnormalities listed on the SMT test report cited above (e.g., blacktopped surface).[247] Samsung said that "without knowing the conditions under which the components were used and/or stored, *it is not possible to project the reliability* of a semiconductor that was manufactured over ten years previously . . .."[248]

Lockheed Martin did not formally notify the Air Force of the suspect counterfeit chip in the C-130J. However, company engineers raised the issue with personnel from the Air Force C-130 program office in a November 22, 2010 conference call.[249] A write-up of the call states that "[Lockheed Martin] and L3 do not believe this is an issue."[250] There is no indication in the write-up of the call that Lockheed Martin mentioned anything about the long-term reliability of the part.[251] Moreover, despite the statement in the SMT test report that said the chips were "suspect counterfeit" and "not considered to be factory original parts," Lockheed Martin's representatives apparently told the Air Force engineers that the "chips have been tested and found to be authentic but re-marked."[252] That distinction was apparently later repeated by Lockheed Martin personnel, leaving the Air Force with the false impression that the memory chip was not a counterfeit.[253] As late as September 2011, Stephen Horvath, Lockheed Martin's Chief Engineer for the C-130 advised the lead Air Force engineer for the C-130 that the part was "mismarked."[254] When asked by the Committee, Mr. Horvath could not explain what it meant to be mismarked or who might have been responsible for the mismarking.[255]

b. *"Six Month" Monitoring Exercise*

Following the initial disclosure from Lockheed Martin's engineers to the Air Force's C-130J engineers, Lockheed Martin agreed to "monitor the failure rate of these [display units] in the field for six months and report results to [the Air Force's] SPO [system program office]."[256] The target for completing that monitoring exercise was May 23, 2011.[257] On May 11, 2011, emails show that engineers from Lockheed Martin began trying to gather information that would reflect six months of monitoring.[258]

---

[246] Hearing to Receive Testimony on Ballistic Missile Defense Policies and Programs in Review of the Defense Authorization Request for Fiscal Year 2012 and the Future Years Defense Program, LTG Patrick J. O'Reilly answers to questions for the record (April 13, 2011).

[247] Letter from Senators Carl Levin and John McCain to Charlie Bae (October 20, 2011).

[248] Letter from Terrence Cross to Senators Carl Levin and John McCain (November 7, 2011) (emphasis added).

[249] Lockheed Martin, *CE Call Agenda 22 November 2010* (November 22, 2010).

[250] *Ibid.*

[251] *Ibid.*

[252] *Ibid.*

[253] Committee Staff briefing with U.S. Air Force (September 20, 2011).

[254] Committee Staff interview of Stephen Horvath (October 18, 2011) at 83-85.

[255] *Ibid.* at 83-90.

[256] Email from Girish Patel to Brian Washington (May 11, 2011).

[257] *Ibid.*

[258] *Ibid.*

Lockheed Martin's engineers reviewed spreadsheets identifying each failure of a display unit from October 2010 to March 2011. Those spreadsheets included short descriptions of the failure (e.g., "failed in flight, no display"), an analysis, and a corrective action. But the spreadsheets were not complete. They included several failures which were identified as "open," meaning that the cause of the failure had not yet been identified.[259] In one example of an "open" or "unresolved" entry, dated February 21, 2011, the chart said "failed in flight, dead display."[260] That is notable given that L-3 Display Systems identified "degraded visual imagery," "blank screen," and "loss of display" as possible results of the suspect counterfeit part's failure.[261] In fact, Lockheed Martin's Electronics Engineering Manager acknowledged that the "failed in flight, dead display" failure could "certainly" be attributable to a failure of the suspect counterfeit memory chip.[262] However, Lockheed Martin produced no documents indicating efforts by the company to determine why that particular display unit, or others, had failed.[263] Nevertheless, Lockheed Martin reported to the Air Force that "no failures from Jan 2011 – June 2011 were attributed to suspect lot."[264]

The company's ability to collect data for the Air Force may have been hindered by the fact that Lockheed Martin had not actually tracked which C-130Js were affected by the suspect counterfeit memory chips. Despite that fact that the SMT Corp. test report clearly stated that the chip was "suspect counterfeit,"[265] because of blacktopping and other reasons, Lockheed Martin explained in a response to the Committee that "the suspect parts were in fact conforming product that unfortunately had the manufacturing/date codes mislabeled. As such, there were no aircraft affected by counterfeit parts and so there was no need to track parts to the aircraft level."[266]

3. Suspect Counterfeit Memory Chip in the C-27J

When L-3 Display Systems learned of the counterfeit chip in November 2010, it filed an L-3 Counterfeit Parts History card, which includes information such as the part's manufacturer, the part number, the supplier, a summary of the counterfeit "incident," and pictures of the counterfeit part.[267] According to Mr. Rick Roelecke, L-3 Communication's Corporate Counterfeit Team Lead, Counterfeit Parts History cards are filed on the internal L-3

---

[259] *See, e.g., L-3 Field Repairs CMDU 5-17-11 (Oct 10-Mar 11)* (May 17, 2011).

[260] *Ibid.*; Committee Staff interview of Brian Washington (September 28, 2011) at 68.

[261] *See, e.g.,* L-3 Display Systems, *Notification to Lockheed Martin* (November 2010), attached to email from Chris Durre to David Stathem and Cynthia Zeigler (November 11, 2010).

[262] Committee Staff interview of Brian Washington (September 28, 2011) at 69.

[263] Lockheed Martin's Electronics Engineering Manager, who was copied on the emails relating to the six-month monitoring exercise, said that he was unaware of any documents that reflected an effort by the company to further investigate the cause of failures identified on the chart. *Ibid.* at 73-74.

[264] Lockheed Martin, *CE Call Agenda 11 July 2011* (undated). The Committee does not know whether the referenced failure or any of the other failures are related to the suspect counterfeit part.

[265] SMT Corporation, *Component Inspection Analysis 00003485 and 00003485A* (November 9, 2010).

[266] Lockheed Martin answers to (August 8, 2011) written questions from Committee Staff (August 16, 2011). At the time that Lockheed Martin's engineers began collecting information to satisfy the Air Force's request, the ability to track the suspect counterfeit parts to the specific assembly was something that the Lockheed engineers noted was lacking, stating, "the MTBFs [mean time between failures] for the [affected display units] cannot be accurately calculated because we do not have enough data to determine the flight hours associated with a specific [display unit] . . . ." Email from Amber Trahan to Brian Washington et al. (May 17, 2011).

[267] *See, e.g.,* L-3 Communications, *Counterfeit Parts History Card for Samsung Part Number KM4216C258G* (undated).

Communications website for "everybody to see," and the "whole purpose" of them is to "share the information across [L-3] divisions."[268]

L-3 Display Systems also filed a report on the Electronic Resellers Association Inc. (ERAI) database, which was required per company policy, and on the Government Industry Data Exchange Program (GIDEP).[269] Both of those databases allow participants to exchange detailed information about suspect counterfeit materials.

In addition, L-3 Display Systems informed its direct customers about the suspect counterfeit part, including Alenia Aeronautica, on December 16, 2010.[270] At that time, however, neither L-3 Display Systems nor Alenia Aeronautica notified L-3 Integrated Systems, the prime contractor to the Air Force for the C-27J. L-3 Display Systems and L-3 Integrated Systems are divisions of the same company, L-3 Communications.

L-3's own personnel found it "surpris[ing]" that the two divisions did not communicate directly about the counterfeit parts.[271] Personnel for L-3 Display Systems said they knew that the display system that they were manufacturing went into the C-27J.[272] They also knew that L-3 Integrated Systems was the prime contractor to the Air Force, since the companies had previously worked together to remove another counterfeit chip which was also integrated into the C-27J.[273]

L-3 Integrated Systems had access to the internal website containing the Counterfeit Parts History card, as well as the reports L-3 Display Systems filed with ERAI and GIDEP. The chief engineer for the C-27J at L-3 Integrated Systems said, however, that his division did not know the suspect counterfeit parts had been used in the C-27J.[274] As a result, L-3 Integrated Systems did not notify the Air Force that over 30 display units with the suspect counterfeit parts had been installed on eight C-27Js, including two C-27Js deployed to Afghanistan, until September 19, 2011 – nearly a year after it had been discovered and just one day before Committee staff was scheduled to meet with the Air Force's C-27J program office on the issue.[275]

When they finally did notify the Air Force about the suspect counterfeit chip, however, L-3 Integrated Systems did not describe it as "counterfeit" or even "suspect counterfeit." Instead, the company referred to the chip as "suspect."[276] Like Lockheed Martin, personnel from L-3 Integrated Systems told the Air Force that the chips were "mislabeled."[277]

---

[268] According to Mr. Roelecke, filing Counterfeit Parts History cards is now a requirement of L-3 Communication's divisions. Committee Staff interview of Rick Roelecke (October 6, 2011) at 25-28.

[269] ERAI Report (December 17, 2010); GIDEP, Alert N. GG5-A-11-01 (December 20, 2010).

[270] Letter from Michael Simmons to David Hope, *Notification of Suspect Components – Part Number U100582-A000, 4 MB IC VRAM Chip* (December 16, 2010).

[271] Committee Staff interview of J. Gregory Bruich (October 11, 2011) at 54-55; Committee Staff interview of Bruce Coffey (October 13, 2011) at 34.

[272] Committee Staff interview of Robert Hunt (October 13, 2011) at 21-22.

[273] Committee Staff interview of J. Gregory Bruich (October 11, 2011) at 28.

[274] *Ibid.* at 97-98.

[275] Letter from Kimberly Kachura to James Leighty (September 19, 2011); Email from Lt Col James Delong to Ozge Guzelsu et al. (February 17, 2012).

[276] Letter from Kimberly Kachura to James Leighty (September 19, 2011).

[277] Committee Staff interview of J. Gregory Bruich (October 11, 2011) at 91.

According to the Air Force, in the week leading up to their September 20, 2011 meeting with Committee staff, L-3 Integrated Systems advised the Air Force that no display unit failures were attributable to the counterfeit part.[278] According to L-3 Integrated Systems chief engineer Gregory Bruich, the material that he reviewed to make that determination was limited to the C-27J failure reporting, analysis and corrective action system or FRACAS database.[279] The FRACAS database, however, contains limited information about failures and their causes. For example, the description of one display unit failure was "[display unit] failed" and the action taken was "removed and replaced the unit."[280] In fact, Bruich later told the Committee that the assessment he made for the Air Force was "crude" and based on almost no information.[281]

There is no indication L-3 Integrated Systems raised any issues with the Air Force about long-term reliability of the suspect counterfeit chip.

4. Meetings between Committee Staff and the U.S. Air Force Program Offices for the C-130J and C-27J

As described above, in the course of the investigation, the Committee received a significant amount of information about suspect counterfeit parts in the C-130J and C-27J. On September 13, 2011, Committee staff requested a meeting with the relevant Air Force program offices to discuss that information.[282]

The Air Force advised Lockheed Martin and L-3 Communications of the Committee's request and asked for information from the two companies regarding the suspect parts at issue. In response, both contractors provided some information to the Air Force.[283] The chief engineer at L-3 Integrated Systems for the C-27J stated, in fact, that he tried to influence the message the Air Force would deliver to the Committee at the meeting, explaining, "I never believe it's in my customer's best interest to have to go into battle or discussion or debate or engage in any game without knowing what the framework, the rules, the game playing field actually looks like. And I did not believe at the time they even knew what was going on."[284]

Committee staff met with Air Force personnel on September 20, 2011. During the course of that meeting, it appeared that the Air Force was not aware of significant information regarding the suspect counterfeit parts.[285] In a subsequent meeting, Air Force personnel were able to review documents that had been provided to the Committee relating to the suspect counterfeit parts. At that meeting, Air Force personnel expressed surprise and disappointment that they had not been provided information by L-3 Communications or Lockheed Martin that they considered

---

[278] Committee Staff briefing with U.S. Air Force (September 20, 2011).
[279] Committee Staff interview of J. Gregory Bruich (October 11, 2011) at 77.
[280] C-27J FRACAS Report No. 0469 (Entry Date: May 3, 2010).
[281] Committee Staff interview of J. Gregory Bruich (October 11, 2011) at 90.
[282] Email from Ilona Cohen to Lt Col James DeLong (September 13, 2011).
[283] Committee Staff briefing with U.S. Air Force (September 30, 2011).
[284] Committee Staff interview of J. Gregory Bruich (October 11, 2011) at 115.
[285] Committee Staff briefing with U.S. Air Force (September 20, 2011).

critical to judging the severity of the counterfeit problem and making informed decisions about how to address it.[286] For example:

- According to the Air Force, neither Lockheed Martin nor L-3 Communications shared pertinent information regarding the reliability and performance of the suspect counterfeit parts, including the independent test report showing the part to be "suspect counterfeit."

- Despite representations by Lockheed Martin and L-3 Communications that there had been no increase in display unit failures attributable to the suspect counterfeit part, according to the Air Force, neither contractor had reviewed sufficient data to come to that determination.

- Lockheed Martin represented to the Air Force that it had conducted six months of "monitoring" of the display units to determine whether the suspect counterfeit parts were causing increased failures. Prior to being advised by Committee staff, the Air Force did not know that the data reviewed by Lockheed Martin was incomplete.

- While Lockheed Martin told the Air Force that the suspect counterfeit parts were "functionally compliant" to authentic genuine parts, the Air Force was apparently not informed that the failure rate of the part had tripled during acceptance and environmental stress testing.[287]

Since the Committee's November 8, 2011 hearing and public release of information about the suspect counterfeit chips in the C-130J and C-27J aircraft, the Air Force has had several conversations with Lockheed Martin and L-3 Communications about the suspect counterfeit chips. According to a December 22, 2011 letter to Chairman Levin, the Air Force has said that they are "aggressively taking action to rectify the breakdowns in communication, remove the parts in question, audit the associated supply chains, and ensure the responsible parties bear the financial burden of replacement."[288] The Air Force has said "[it] is removing all of the affected parts from the fleet and supply chain. While our engineers remain confident that the parts do not create flight safety risks, they are concerned about long-term reliability and supply chain vulnerability."[289] As of March 2012, however, Lockheed Martin had removed and replaced only a handful of the display units in the C-130Js that are affected by the suspect counterfeit memory chip.[290] Also as of March 2012, less than a quarter of the affected display units in the C-27Js had been repaired or replaced.[291]

---

[286] Committee Staff briefing with U.S. Air Force (October 21, 2011).
[287] Committee Staff briefing with U.S. Air Force (September 20, 2011); Committee Staff briefing with U.S. Air Force (October 21, 2011).
[288] Letter from Anthony Reardon to Senator Carl Levin (December 22, 2011).
[289] *Ibid.*
[290] Email from Lt Col James DeLong to Ilona Cohen (March 12, 2012).
[291] U.S. Air Force Fact Sheet (March 16, 2012).

41

5. Hong Dark Electronic Trade

The suspect counterfeit electronic parts used in the C-130J and C-27J airplanes originated with a company in Shenzhen, China, called Hong Dark Electronic Trade Company (Hong Dark). Hong Dark sold the parts at issue to Global IC Trading Group, an independent distributor in the U.S. Global IC Trading Group sold the parts to L-3 Communications Display Systems.

   a. Chinese Parts Flow From Hong Dark Electronic Trade to the Military Supply Chain through Global IC Trading Group and L-3 Communications

In February 2009, Global IC Trading Group issued a purchase order to Hong Dark for 4,500 pieces of a memory chip manufactured by Samsung.[292] On its purchase order, Global IC Trading Group advised Hong Dark: "[C]ustomer will only take the 4500 pieces if the samples are approved."[293] Shortly after that purchase order was issued, Hong Dark selected 18 pieces as a sample and sent it to Global IC Trading Group for testing.[294] Global IC Trading Group sent two of those parts to Oneida Research Services for analysis. Oneida's testing revealed "no anomalies" with the parts.[295] Based on Oneida's testing results for those two pieces – which came from the 18 piece sample selected by Hong Dark – Global IC Trading Group purchased and received 4,500 pieces of the Samsung memory chip from Hong Dark in March and April 2009.[296] In May of 2009, Global IC Trading Group placed another order with Hong Dark for sale to L-3 Display Systems for approximately 6,000 more of the same Samsung memory chips.[297] As discussed above, the memory chips supplied by Hong Dark were subsequently determined to be suspect counterfeit.

The Samsung memory chip in the display units was not the first counterfeit part that L-3 Display Systems had received from Hong Dark Electronic Trade through Global IC Trading Group. Hong Dark was also the source of counterfeit parts discovered by L-3 Display Systems in October 2009. In that case, L-3 Display Systems was informed by Lattice, the purported manufacturer, that a part that was integrated into display units on military airplanes, had "not [been] built by any Lattice assembly subcontractors."[298] However, L-3 Display Systems did not learn at that time that Hong Dark had supplied the part to Global IC Trading Group. In fact, it was not until November 2010, when L-3 Display Systems discovered that the Samsung memory chip was counterfeit, that it finally learned that Hong Dark had supplied both the Lattice part and the Samsung part.[299]

In November 2010, Global IC Trading Group notified L-3 Display Systems that they had also supplied the company with a third lot of parts from Hong Dark.[300] Despite issuing a part

---

[292] Global IC Trading Group, *Purchase Order N. 13258* (February 12, 2009).
[293] *Ibid.*
[294] Global IC Trading Group, *Receiving Report N. 7249* (February 18, 2009, updated March 17, 2009).
[295] Oneida Research Services, *Counterfeit Screening Report N. 180883-001* (February 24, 2009).
[296] Global IC Trading Group, *Receiving Report N. 7249* (February 18, 2009, updated March 17, 2009).
[297] Global IC Trading Group, *Purchase Order N. 13476* (May 14, 2009); Global IC Trading Group, *Receiving Report N. 7436* (May 29, 2009).
[298] Letter from Thomas J. Lawler to Robert T. Hunt (November 5, 2009); L-3 Display Systems, *Evaluation of Lattice ispLSI 1048E 90LQ LPN U100188-000* (October 28, 2009).
[299] Email from Paul Meyers to Robert Hunt et al. (November 10, 2010).
[300] *Ibid.*

purge notification, which quarantined those parts in their own inventory, L-3 Display Systems did not recall the parts from that third lot that had already been fielded in display units.[301] Nor did the company send the Hong Dark-supplied parts for counterfeit analysis or notify its customers that the parts were suspect counterfeit.[302] As a result, some of those parts were installed on display units intended for the EA-6B military aircraft.[303] L-3 finally submitted parts from that third lot for testing in October 2011. The company did so only after Committee staff asked about the parts in interviews with personnel from L-3 Display Systems.[304] The testing that resulted from those inquires identified the parts as "suspect counterfeit."[305]

In testimony before the Committee, L-3 Communications Vice President for Corporate Procurement, Mr. Ralph DeNino, acknowledged that the company had made a mistake in failing to test a part that was known to have come from a source that had previously provided the company with counterfeits. When asked why it took so long to test the third part, Mr. DeNino said: "there is no real good answer on that other than the parts should have been tested and we did not."[306]

Global IC Trading Group's procurements from Hong Dark were not limited to three lots of counterfeit parts. In June 2011, the Committee asked the company to provide a list of all of the parts supplied to it by Hong Dark in 2009 and 2010.[307] Global IC's response revealed that Hong Dark made nearly 30 shipments of approximately 20 different lots of parts in 2009 and 2010.[308] In total, more than 28,000 electronic parts from Hong Dark were supplied to Global IC Trading Group, and in turn sold to divisions of L-3 Communications.[309] Prior to being advised by the Committee, L-3 Communications was unaware that Hong Dark was the source of those parts.[310] Nor had the company asked Global IC Trading Group for that information, something that the L-3 Corporate Vice President for Procurement, Mr. Ralph DeNino, admitted "we should have done . . . on our own."[311]

As of the Committee's November 8, 2011 hearing, L-3 Communications did not know where all the parts from Hong Dark were or have an accounting of all the military systems that

---

[301] Committee Staff interview of Robert Hunt (October 13, 2011) at 76; SASC Hearing at 105-06.

[302] Committee Staff interview of Robert Hunt (October 13, 2011) at 76; SASC Hearing at 105-06.

[303] Letter from Jack Deschauer to Senators Carl Levin and John McCain (January 4, 2012).

[304] Committee Staff interview of Ralph DeNino (October 24, 2011) at 36-38.

[305] SMT Corporation, *Component Inspection Analysis N. 00006407* (October 14, 2011).

[306] Mr. DeNino also described the corrective actions that L-3 Communications was taking in response to that mistake. SASC Hearing at 106.

[307] The Committee sent request letters to several independent distributors asking for a chart listing each occasion in 2009 and 2010 on which the independent distributor purchased electronic parts from an individual or company known to have provided at least one suspect counterfeit part in that same time period. *See, e.g.*, letter from Senators Carl Levin and John McCain to Lori LeRoy (June 7, 2011).

[308] Letter from Lori Leroy to Ilona Cohen, re: Response to U.S. Senate Armed Services Committee letter dated June 7, 2011 (June 24, 2011); Global IC, *Parts Supplied to L-3 Sources from Hong Dark Electronic Trade* (June 24, 2011).

[309] Letter from Lori Leroy to Ilona Cohen, re: Response to U.S. Senate Armed Services Committee letter dated June 7, 2011 (June 24, 2011); Global IC, *Parts Supplied to L-3 Sources from Hong Dark Electronic Trade* (June 24, 2011).

[310] SASC Hearing at 105-06.

[311] *Ibid.* at 107.

might be affected by the suspect counterfeit parts.[312] Ralph DeNino testified that the company was "scrambling" to determine how all the parts from Hong Dark had been used on L-3's systems.[313]

After the hearing, L-3 Communications sent samples of each of those approximately 20 different lots of parts to independent laboratories for counterfeit testing. According to an attorney for L-3 Communications, "testing was performed on all the parts from November 2011 through early 2012" and the "testing houses identified *all but two* of the parts as suspect counterfeit."[314] After the hearing, L-3 Communications also provided the Committee with a list of dozens of L-3 systems that contained the suspect counterfeit parts that had been supplied by Hong Dark, and were either installed on or were intended for use on military equipment.[315] The list of military equipment affected by the suspect counterfeit parts is extensive. Parts from Hong Dark made it into L-3's Traffic Alert and Collision Avoidance Systems (TCAS) intended for the C-5AMP, C-12, and the Global Hawk. According to the Federal Aviation Administration, TCAS was "designed to increase cockpit awareness of proximate aircraft and to serve as a 'last line of defense' for the prevention of mid-air collisions."[316] In addition, parts from Hong Dark made it into assemblies intended for the P-3, the Special Operations Force A/MH-6M, and other military equipment, like the Excalibur (an extended range artillery projectile), the Navy Integrated Submarine Imaging System, and the Army Stryker Mobile Gun.[317]

b. Additional Chinese Parts Flow From Hong Dark Electronic Trade to L-3 Communications Through Global IC Trading Group

L-3 Communications was not the only military contractor to have bought parts supplied by Hong Dark Electronic Trade. In response to the Committee's request for information, Global IC Trading Group identified all sales of electronic parts that it had acquired from Hong Dark.[318] In that response, Global IC stated that it had sold more than 42,000 such parts to Lockheed Martin. In March 2012, Lockheed Martin advised the Committee that it purchased those parts pursuant to an agreement to procure parts for L-3 Communications East, a business that L-3 had acquired from Lockheed Martin in 1997.[319] In March 2012, a lawyer for L-3 Communications reported that some of these electronic parts were rejected and returned to Global IC Trading Group, some parts were received but not used, and some parts were determined to be authentic.[320]

According to the Air Force, "approximately 84,000 suspect counterfeit electronic parts purchased from Hong Dark entered the DOD supply chain, and many of these parts have been

---

[312] *Ibid.* at 107-08.

[313] *Ibid.* at 106.

[314] Letter from Jack Deschauer to Senators Carl Levin and John McCain, re: Global IC Trading Group Parts Supplied to L-3 Sourced from Hong Dark Electronics Trade (March 2, 2012) (emphasis added).

[315] Letter from Jack Deschauer to Senators Carl Levin and John McCain (January 4, 2012).

[316] Federal Aviation Administration, TCAS Home Page, *available at* http://adsb.tc.faa.gov/TCAS.htm (last visited March 13, 2012).

[317] Letter from Jack Deschauer to Senators Carl Levin and John McCain (January 4, 2012).

[318] Letter from Lori Leroy to Ilona Cohen, re: Response to U.S. Senate Armed Services Committee letter dated June 7, 2011 (June 24, 2011).

[319] Email from Jay Brozost to Ilona Cohen et al. (March 1, 2012).

[320] Email from Jack Deschauer to Ilona Cohen et al. (March 16, 2012)

installed on DOD aircraft."[321]   According to the Air Force, those parts all made their way into the DOD supply chain through Global IC Trading Group.[322]   The Committee does not know how many other companies in the defense supply chain may have used Hong Dark Electronic Trade as a source of electronic parts.   On January 13, 2012, the Air Force issued a notice of suspension to Hong Dark Electronic Trade and Global IC Trading Group.[323]   As of April 18, 2012, Hong Dark was listed on the Excluded Parties List System (EPLS), making it ineligible to compete for future government contracts or subcontracts.[324]   Global IC Trading Group was not listed on the EPLS as the Air Force terminated the company's suspension on April 13, 2012.[325]

D. Suspect Counterfeit Parts in U.S. Navy's P-8A Poseidon

The P-8A Poseidon is a Boeing 737 airplane modified to incorporate anti-submarine and anti-surface warfare capabilities. As of October 2011, three P-8A flight test aircraft were in test at the Naval Air Station at Patuxent River, Maryland and the Navy intends to purchase a total of 117 P-8A aircraft from Boeing.[326]

BAE Systems is a subcontractor to Boeing on the P-8A and manufactures an Ice Detection System Logic Module Assembly used on the airplane's flight deck.[327]   The module is installed on all P-8A Poseidon aircraft.[328]   The ice detection module receives inputs from the airplane's ice detector probe and indicates via a warning light when the probe detects ice on the aircraft's exterior.[329]   The ice detection module contains two identical circuit cards, each of which includes a military grade field programmable gate array (FPGA) manufactured by Xilinx, a large semiconductor manufacturer that specializes in programmable devices.[330]   While Boeing has said that failure of the part would not pose a safety risk, the two FPGAs host the module's logic functions and, if either were to fail, the module itself would not work properly and a fault light on the module would indicate a malfunction.[331]

On August 17, 2011 Boeing sent a message to the U.S. Navy's P-8A program office stating, "[i]t is suspected that the [ice detection] module may be a reworked part that should not have been put on the airplane originally and should be replaced immediately."[332]   Boeing's

---

[321] Department of the Air Force, *Memorandum in support of the suspension of Hong Dark Electronic Trade Company* (January 13, 2012) at 2.

[322] *Ibid.*

[323] Department of the Air Force, *Memorandum in support of the suspension of Hong Dark Electronic Trade Company* (January 13, 2012).

[324] Committee staff search of Excluded Parties List System (last executed April 18, 2012).

[325] Letter from Steven A. Shaw, Deputy General Counsel, USAF to Global IC Trading Group, LLC (April 13, 2012).

[326] Email from Louise Vitale to Joe Bryan (October 28, 2011); Email from Louise Vitale to Joe Bryan (November 2, 2011).

[327] BAE Systems, *Ice Detection System Logic Module Assembly (P5-83)* (December 23, 2009).

[328] BAE Systems, *Ice Detection System Logic Module Assembly (P5-83) Obsolescence* (undated).

[329] Boeing answers to written questions from Committee Staff (August 5, 2011); Boeing White Paper to the Senate Armed Services Committee (November 2011) at 4-5.

[330] A field programmable gate array is a type of integrated circuit that may be programmed after it is manufactured. The part number for the Xilinx PGA in the ice detection module is XC3042A-7PG84M.

[331] Boeing White Paper to the Senate Armed Services Committee (November 2011) at 5.

[332] Boeing Vector Message, re: "Ice Detection Module Assembly" (August 17, 2011). Boeing later said that the message was:

message was sent more than a year and a half after the company found out about the suspect parts and only after multiple inquiries from the Committee.

1. BAE Seeks Parts to Support P-8A Production

In January 2003, Xilinx issued notice that they were discontinuing production of a number of FPGAs. The company subsequently stopped manufacturing the parts, which included an FPGA used in the manufacture of ice detection modules used on some Boeing 737 airplanes.[333] In November 2008, there were discussions at BAE about the need to secure a sufficient supply of the Xilinx FPGAs to support BAE's contract with Boeing to manufacture ice detection modules for the Navy's P-8A airplane, a derivative of the 737.[334]

At that time, BAE Systems had an arrangement with Tandex Test Labs, a California-based company that conducts testing on electronic parts, whereby Tandex would act as both the supplier and the test lab for parts that BAE needed but were no longer in production.[335] Tandex identified the Xilinx parts BAE needed to build the ice detection modules and, in November 2008, sent BAE samples of the parts it purchased from Abacus Technologies, a Florida-based independent distributor.[336] Later that month, Tandex alerted BAE to the availability of 300 additional Xilinx FPGAs, also from Abacus.[337]

It is not clear that Tandex knew where Abacus had bought the parts. An email from an Abacus employee to Tandex implied that the parts had come from an original equipment manufacturer (OEM), not a distributor.[338] Documents also suggest that Tandex believed that Abacus's supplier was located in Germany.[339] Abacus, however, had purchased the Xilinx parts from a company called A Access (Japan) Electronics, an affiliate of A Access Electronics (Hong Kong) Limited, and wired payment for the parts to an account at the Chartered Bank Shenzhen in Shenzhen, China.[340]

"issued solely in response to [the Senate Armed Services] Committee inquiry about the [ice detection module] and to assuage any possible U.S. Navy concern. The Vector message used the terms 'Critical' and 'should be replaced immediately' due to the scrutiny that this part had received, not due to any safety or functionality concern."

Boeing did not explain why the suspect counterfeit Xilinx devices were put on the plane when the notice stated that they "should not have been put on the airplane originally." Boeing White Paper to the Senate Armed Services Committee (November 2011) at 9.

[333] Xilinx Inc., *Product Discontinuation Notice PDN2003-01* (January 17, 2003).

[334] Email from Brian Jurusik to Rex Johnson et al. (November 20, 2008).

[335] Committee Staff interview of Rex Johnson (October 3, 2011) at 16-17.

[336] Email from Rex Johnson to Brian Peale et al. (November 10, 2008); BAE Purchase Order N. 124068 to Tandex Test Labs (October 16, 2008).

[337] Email from Sonia Medrano to Rex Johnson (November 21, 2008); Email from Chris Anaya to Sonia Medrano (December 12, 2008).

[338] Email from Chris Anaya to Sonia Medrano (December 12, 2008).

[339] BAE Purchase Order N. 124068 to Tandex Test Labs (October 16, 2008).

[340] Email from Dave MacDougall to Joe Bryan (August 22, 2011).

2. Tandex Identifies "Anomalous Conditions"- BAE Requests Testing

On November 25, 2008, Tandex President Brian Peale emailed BAE that Tandex had identified "anomalous conditions" with some of the Xilinx parts his company had bought from Abacus, stating, "we don't believe any of these are rejectable but wanted to make you aware."[341] After reviewing pictures of the anomalies, a BAE engineer replied, "[t]hey all looked to me that they had been removed from some [printed wiring assemblies] in this case they are refurbished and we do not use refurbished parts."[342]

The following day, that same BAE engineer emailed a company buyer regarding the planned purchase from Tandex, stating, "Please ask Tandex to perform 100% visual inspection and select parts that do not have . . . anomalous conditions for us."[343] The BAE buyer forwarded the email to Tandex along with a document requesting that Tandex visually inspect and measure the physical dimensions of "100%" of the parts intended for BAE.[344]

On December 10, 2008, BAE approved an Advance Sale Order (ASO) to purchase the parts.[345] The ASO stated that "all parts will be purchased from brokers and screened by Tandex Test Labs."[346] Two days later, BAE issued a purchase order to Tandex for 250 of those parts. The purchase order included a $1,500 payment to Tandex for screening the parts.[347]

3. Tandex Delivers Xilinx FPGAs to BAE

In January 2009, Tandex delivered a tranche of 50 Xilinx FPGAs to BAE. A Tandex test report indicated that the company had visually inspected the parts at 40 times magnification, had tested them for their resistance to solvents, and had verified their physical dimensions.[348]

Tandex delivered additional tranches of 50 Xilinx parts in February, March, April, May, and June 2009. Each of those deliveries included a Certificate of Conformance (CoC) indicating that Tandex had processed 50 parts and that all 50 had passed.[349] The CoCs also contained the following statement, signed by a Tandex employee:

"I hereby certify that the subject components have been processed and inspected in accordance with instructions with specifications referenced in your purchase

---

[341] Email from Brian Peale to Rex Johnson et al. (November 25, 2008).

[342] Email from Kim Nguyen to Brian Peale et al. (November 25, 2008).

[343] Email from Kim Nguyen to Rex Johnson (November 26, 2008).

[344] Email from Rex Johnson to Sonia Medrano et al. (November 26, 2008).

[345] BAE Systems, *Advance Sales Order/Stock Order* (December 10, 2008).

[346] *Ibid.*

[347] BAE Systems Purchase Order N. 128235 (December 12, 2008). Following approval of the ASO, BAE issued two purchase orders to Tandex for a total of 300 of the Xilinx parts. The parts were to be supplied to BAE in tranches of 50 over a period of several months. BAE Systems Purchase Orders N. 128235 & 128245 (December 11, 12, 2008).

[348] Tandex Test Labs, *Test Report Job N. BOI-573-03-A* (January 12, 2009).

[349] Tandex Test Labs, *Certificates of Conformance* (February 10, 2009, March 5, 2009, April 13, 2009, May 18, 2009 & June 15, 2009). The CoCs stated that the method of testing Tandex used was BAE's Platform Solutions Procurement Procedure (PSPP). The PSPP describes BAE's requirements for purchasing goods and services from an approved supplier.

order. Physical records and/or date pertinent to applicable military, proprietary, and/or commercial specifications are on file and available upon request for inspection at this facility."[350]

Once received at BAE, the parts were subjected to electrical testing. BAE did not perform other testing such as visual inspection and measuring the parts' dimensions, however, as those were to have been already completed by Tandex per an agreement between the two companies. BAE used parts supplied by Tandex to construct ice detection modules, eight of which were delivered to Boeing. One of those ice detection modules was installed on a P-8A Poseidon airplane intended for the U.S. Navy and the remaining seven were installed on 737 airplanes destined for Boeing commercial customers.[351]

4. Problem on Boeing Flight Line

In late November 2009, a BAE Systems Emergent Response Team was called to Boeing's flight line when a Boeing technician "heard something rattling around inside the [ice detection] module."[352] When the module was removed from the plane, the technician realized that a Xilinx FPGA had "fallen out of the socket."[353] The discovery prompted an investigation by BAE.

BAE pulled its inventory and conducted a visual inspection of 249 Xilinx parts held in Irving, Texas. That inspection revealed a large number of anomalies, including parts with different ceramic body sizes and different size metal tabs. Parts showed signs of having been sanded down and resurfaced. Pin lengths were different and did not meet manufacturer specifications. Parts were chipped and dented. FPGAs from four different date codes were represented to be from the same lot. The findings led BAE to conclude that "these symptoms are very characteristic of refurbished/counterfeit parts."[354]

On December 18, 2009, a BAE Sourcing engineer emailed Brian Peale of Tandex, "I hate to be the bearer of bad news, but it appears as though we received refurbished parts from Tandex, which resulted in a field failure on a flight critical piece of hardware."[355] BAE asked Tandex for help in determining "the process breakdown that allowed these parts to pass the screening measures requested."[356]

A few days later, BAE got test results on 50 additional Xilinx parts the company had purchased from Tandex. Those 50 parts showed many of the same anomalies as the first 249. In addition, some of the FPGAs were of different colors, had different fonts in their markings, and

---

[350] *Ibid.* Just as in the January tranche, the CoCs indicated the method of testing Tandex used was BAE's Platform Solutions Procurement Procedure.

[351] Email from Theotonius Rozario to Murray Hall et al. (March 30, 2011).

[352] Email from Ray Orton to Donna Graves et al. (November 30, 2009); BAE Systems, *Ice Detection System Logic Module Assembly (P5-83)* (December 23, 2009); BAE Systems, *Material Alert* (May 24, 2011).

[353] Email from Ray Orton to Donna Graves et al. (November 30, 2009); BAE Systems, *Ice Detection System Logic Module Assembly (P5-83)* (December 23, 2009).

[354] Email from Hanna A. Kanciak-Chwialkowski to Murrray Hall (December 14, 2009).

[355] Email from Carrie Mizell to Brian Peale et al. (December 18, 2009) (emphasis in original).

[356] *Ibid.*

had text that was off-center. Others had bent leads and one part was missing a lead altogether. Parts also showed "noticeable sanding marks."[357] A BAE component engineer stated simply, "They don't look good."[358]

5. BAE Alerts Boeing About Suspect Counterfeit Parts

On December 23, 2009, BAE alerted Boeing's Procurement Agent for the ice detection modules that it had found evidence that the Xilinx parts supplied by Tandex had been "reworked."[359] On January 7, 2010 the company issued a formal Notification of Escape (NOE) to Boeing indicating that eight ice detection modules contained "suspect components."[360] The NOE called the parts "unacceptable for use" and listed "inconsistencies" with the parts, including that they had "repainted metal tabs," "signs of resurfacing," "bent leads," "peeling coating," and "nicks and dents on surface of pins."[361] BAE recommended "replacement of the suspect components" and provided a list of eight ice detection modules BAE had delivered to Boeing containing suspect parts.[362] In an email a few days later, a BAE engineer explained to colleagues the basis for the recommendation stating, "even though [the parts] are working, there is a reliability risk."[363]

On February 11, 2010, Boeing itself issued an internal report called a "Suspect Discrepancy Report" (SDR) describing the problem. The SDR listed eight aircraft affected by the suspect counterfeit parts and stated, "there is evidence that the component purchased by BAE Systems beginning in December 2008, are reworked parts and unacceptable for use."[364] The SDR listed the anomalies identified in BAE's notification and stated that "BAE recommends removing and replacing suspect components."[365]

6. Tandex Response to BAE Systems Corrective Action

Coincidentally, the same day that Boeing issued its SDR, Tandex President Brian Peale responded to BAE's request for an explanation as to how the counterfeit parts had made it through Tandex's screening. Mr. Peale told BAE that, aside from the first 50 Xilinx parts his company had delivered to BAE in January 2009, Tandex had not actually tested any of the devices shipped to BAE. He said that Tandex had only counted the parts and conducted what he called a "minor visual" exam before shipping them to BAE.[366]

---

[357] Email from Benjamin Franze to Hanna A. Kanciak-Chwialkowski (December 21, 2009).
[358] *Ibid.*
[359] Email from Brian Jurisik to Theotonius Rozario et al. (December 23, 2009); In November 2011, Boeing advised the Committee that until alerted by the Committee's background memo regarding the investigation and the November 8, 2011 hearing, it was unaware that Tandex had supplied 250 FPGAs to BAE without inspecting them.
[360] BAE Systems, *Notification of Escape* (January 7, 2010).
[361] *Ibid.*
[362] *Ibid.*
[363] Email from Murry Hall to Gary Hotchkin et al. (January 11, 2020).
[364] Boeing, *Suspect Discrepancy Report* (February 11, 2010).
[365] *Ibid.*
[366] Tandex Test Labs, *Corrective Action Form QMF 06 rev. A* (February 11, 2010).

As to why his company did not conduct testing, Mr. Peale claimed that Tandex "was led to believe" that BAE would "perform visual and mechanical inspection" of the parts.[367] He acknowledged, however, that Tandex "had no documentation supporting this assumption."[368]

Rex Johnson, a BAE senior buyer who dealt with Tandex on the purchase of the Xilinx parts said that he did not recall ever telling Mr. Peale that BAE would conduct visual and mechanical inspection of the parts. Mr. Johnson said that he did not even have the authority to change BAE's agreement with Tandex to allow for that and that such a change "would've had to come to [BAE] in writing. It would've had to have gone through the engineering group. The engineering manager would've had to approve it. There would be a signature trail."[369] In response to a Committee request, BAE found "no documents indicating that BAE Systems would assume responsibility" for that testing.[370]

All relevant documents reviewed by the Committee suggest that Tandex was responsible for that testing and, other than Mr. Peale's statement, the Committee has not identified any evidence to suggest that anyone at BAE advised Tandex that BAE would assume that responsibility.

Mr. Peale also claimed that "miscommunication between BAE and Tandex" caused him to misunderstand what testing he was to conduct.[371] He claimed that Tandex had received "confusing work instructions" from BAE and believed it was "BAE's job" to inspect the parts.[372] Tandex had, however, previously performed testing for BAE under work instructions identical to those that Peale identified as confusing. When asked why he had completed the testing under those identical work instructions, Mr. Peale stated "we weren't confused at that time."[373]

BAE paid Tandex $1,500 to screen the Xilinx parts. Asked whether such a charge was appropriate given that Tandex failed to test most of the parts, Mr. Peale stated Tandex "should not have charged" BAE for the screening it failed to conduct.[374] While BAE removed Tandex as an approved supplier to screen parts purchased from independent distributors, as of September 2011, Tandex remained an authorized supplier to Boeing and conducted testing and parts assembly for BAE.[375]

7. BAE Presses Boeing to Replace Suspect Counterfeits

A Boeing service engineer said that he received Boeing's February 11, 2010 Suspect Discrepancy Report (SDR) and the BAE notification of escape (NOE) describing the suspect counterfeit Xilinx FPGAs around the time the SDR was issued.[376] The role of Boeing service

---

[367] *Ibid.*

[368] *Ibid.*

[369] Committee Staff interview of Rex Johnson (October 3, 2011) at 59-61.

[370] BAE Systems answers to August 3, 2011 written questions from Committee Staff (August 12, 2011).

[371] Tandex Test Labs, *Corrective Action Form QMF 06 rev. A* (February 11, 2010).

[372] Committee Staff interview of Brian Peale (October 17, 2011) at 20, 22.

[373] *Ibid.* at 39.

[374] *Ibid.* at 43.

[375] BAE Systems, *Notification of Escape* (January 7, 2010); Letter from David Hammond to Senators Carl Levin and John McCain (September 15, 2011); Email from Steve Koh to Ilona Cohen et al. (October 6, 2011).

[376] Committee Staff interview of Robert Kertesz at 9-15.

engineering is to investigate nonconformities (like that identified in the SDR) and determine how the nonconformity should be resolved and whether to notify affected customers.[377] The NOE the Boeing engineer received contained a list of eight ice detection modules affected by the suspect counterfeit FPGAs. As discussed above, one of those ice detection modules was installed on a P-8A Poseidon airplane intended for the U.S. Navy and the remaining seven were installed on 737 aircraft destined for Boeing commercial customers.

On March 2, 2010, BAE's Product Support Program Manager for the ice detection module, emailed Boeing personnel asking about three of the eight aircraft that contained ice detection modules with suspect counterfeits.[378] A Boeing engineer responded that the three aircraft had not yet been delivered to the customers and were "still in Boeing's possession," leading BAE's Product Support Program Manager to suggest that "we should try and corral the suspect hardware and have our ERT team rework them."[379] He asked, "What do we need to do to make that happen?"[380] No action, however, was taken to remove the suspect counterfeit parts at that time.

On March 5, 2010 BAE's Product Support Manager emailed Boeing's service engineer, urging him to send a message to Boeing's customers "describing the situation [with the ice detection modules] and asking them to send their unit in at the next opportunity."[381] Less than a week later, however, the BAE Product Support Manager told the Boeing service engineer that BAE had developed a new configuration to fix the ice detection modules. He said that that fix required BAE to draft a Component Service Bulletin (CSB)[382] and that "[s]ince we have deemed [the suspect counterfeit parts] a long term reliability issue, we feel it would probably be better to wait until the CSB is close to being released before we contact the customer to send their units in."[383]

BAE drafted the CSB and Boeing approved its issuance in June 2010.[384] However, Boeing still did not notify the Navy or its commercial customers that airplanes contained suspect counterfeit parts in their ice detection modules. When asked why Boeing failed to notify its customers, both Boeing's service engineer and the company's procurement agent stated that they believed the BAE CSB constituted notification.[385] It is unclear as to how they arrived at that conclusion. The CSB did not indicate that the ice detection module contained suspect counterfeit parts, nor did it indicate that some ice detection modules contained parts whose reliability was in

---

[377] *Ibid.* at 9; Boeing White Paper to Senate Armed Services Committee (November 2011) at 3-4.

[378] Email from Jackson Wetzel to Robert Kertesz et al. (March 2, 2010).

[379] Email from Jeffrey Look to Jackson Wetzel et al. (March 2, 2010); Email from Jack Wetzel to Theotonius Rozario et al. (March 5, 2010).

[380] Email from Jeffrey Look to Jackson Wetzel et al. (March 2, 2010); Email from Jack Wetzel to Theotonius Rozario et al. (March 5, 2010).

[381] Email from Jack Wetzel to Robert Kertesz (March 5, 2010).

[382] Email from Jackson Wetzel to Robert Kertesz et al. (March 10, 2010). Wetzel later described the CSB to Committee Staff as "a document that authorizes and gives instructions on how to modify a unit." Committee Staff interview of Jackson Wetzel (August 21, 2011) at 14.

[383] Email from Jackson Wetzel to Robert Kertesz et al. (March 10, 2010).

[384] Letter from Theotonius Rozario to Mary Howland, re: "Approval of BAE Systems Component service Bulletin 69-78533-30-02" (June 2, 2010).

[385] Committee Staff interview of Robert Kertesz (September 30, 2011) at 32, 37; Committee Staff interview of Theotonius Rozario (September 27, 2011) at 59.

question.[386] According to BAE's Product Support Manager, the CSB was not even written to address the suspect counterfeit part issue.[387] Rather, its purpose was to alert customers that a modification to the ice detection module had been authorized.[388]

In July 2010, Boeing service engineering closed out its Suspect Discrepancy Report on the suspect counterfeit parts in the ice detection modules indicating "NAR" – no action required. While Boeing acknowledged in the document that the "components may have somewhat lower reliability" it concluded that "the engineering consensus is that the units can remain on the airplane and be repaired on an attrition basis."[389]

As to the three planes identified in March as being in Boeing's possession, they were delivered to customers months later with the suspect counterfeit parts intact – one in June 2010 and two in December 2010.[390] While the Navy P-8A that contained an affected ice detection module was not discussed in the March 2010 exchange, it too had yet to be delivered. According to the Navy, it wasn't until August 13, 2010 that Boeing transferred the P-8A to the Naval Air Station at Patuxent River for flight test operations.[391] By that date, Boeing had known about the suspect counterfeit parts for more than eight months.

8. Senate Armed Services Committee Requests Spurs Discussion

In February 2011, the Committee sent letters to BAE Systems, Boeing and other defense contractors requesting documents and information on suspect counterfeit electronic parts. Those requests gave rise to a series of BAE and Boeing emails relating to the suspect counterfeit parts in the ice detection modules.

On March 30, 2011, Boeing's procurement agent emailed BAE asking whether they had "an obligation to notify the airlines about this [suspect counterfeit] issue and provide a remedy?"[392] The email identified the U.S. Navy and the six other Boeing customers who had received ice detection modules containing suspect counterfeit parts.[393] The following day,

---

[386] BAE Systems, *Service Bulletin Ice Detection System Logic Module Assembly PCA* (June 2, 2010).

[387] Committee Staff interview of Jackson Wetzel (August 21, 2011) at 14, 18-19.

[388] BAE Systems, *Service Bulletin Ice Detection System Logic Module Assembly PCA* (June 2, 2010). Mr. Kertesz later acknowledged that the CSB did not notify Boeing's customers that the affected ice detection modules contained suspect counterfeit parts and agreed that notification would "probably" have been appropriate at the time it was issued. Rozario stated that Boeing should have notified its customers in March 2011. Committee Staff interview of Robert Kertesz (September 30, 2011) at 40; Committee Staff interview of Theotonius Rozario (September 27, 2011) at 67.

[389] Boeing, *SDR Closure Template* (July 2010).

[390] Boeing, *List of aircraft delivered to Boeing customers* (August 1, 2011); Boeing responses to July 28, 2011 Committee Staff written questions (August 8, 2011). The three planes were sent to a Boeing subcontractor for auxiliary tank installation, after which they were placed in storage by Boeing, where they remained until they were delivered to Boeing's customers. Email from Steve Koh to Joe Bryan et al. (October 17, 2011).

[391] Department of Defense Information Paper, re: Multi-Mission Maritime Aircraft (September 14, 2011).

[392] Email from Theotonius Rozario to Murray Hall et al. (March 30, 2011).

[393] The six Boeing customers identified as having received ice detection modules containing suspect counterfeit parts were Dallah Albaraka Company in Jordan, CGP Airplane leased to Ukraine International Airlines (two airplanes leased), KAL Korean Air, Aircraft Operation GMBH in Austria, Purple Holding Management in Saudi Arabia, and Tary Network Limited in the Russian Federation. Email from Theotonius Rozario to Murray Hall et al. (March 30, 2011).

BAE's Product Support Program Manager responded that the units should be returned and the suspect parts replaced.[394] He also reminded Boeing of BAE's January 2010 Notice of Escape which recommended replacement of the suspect components.[395] The Product Support Manager sent a second email to Boeing that same day stating, "I think that [Boeing's service engineer] just needs to notify the operators."[396] Notwithstanding the emails from BAE, months passed without Boeing notifying either the Navy or its commercial customers about the suspect counterfeit parts.

Subsequent Committee inquires prompted additional discussion about the parts. On July 27, 2011, BAE's Product Support Manager emailed Boeing's service engineer and the company's procurement agent, "We have the Senate Armed Services Committee inquiring about [the affected ice detection modules]. Can you confirm that the affected operators were notified?"[397] Following that email, Boeing's service engineer emailed the company's procurement agent that "the disposition was NAR [no action required]. Components may have a somewhat lower reliability, the engineering consensus is that the units can remain on the airplane and be repaired on an attrition basis. . . . We did not alert the customers."[398]

The procurement agent responded, "I see your point, but it might be in our best interest to notify the operators so they can get replacement parts, especially since the P-8A is involved and the U.S. Senate Armed Services Committee is inquiring."[399] Another Boeing engineer also responded, stating, ". . . I do not see why we would not go forward and notify the affected operators."[400] That same day, BAE's Product Support Manager wrote the Boeing procurement agent, "I think the operators should be notified so that they can decide how to handle their impacted hardware."[401]

9. Boeing Notifies the Navy

On August 17, 2011, more than a year and a half after the suspect counterfeit parts were first identified, Boeing sent a message marked "**Priority**: Critical" to the U.S. Navy's P-8A program office. The message said, "It is suspected that the [ice detection] module may be a reworked part that should not have been put on the airplane originally and should be replaced immediately."[402]

Boeing subsequently notified its commercial customers which were sold ice detection modules containing suspect counterfeit parts.[403] A Boeing engineer described that notification in an email to BAE's Product Support Manager, "It was short and sweet, and of course (unlike other elements within Boeing) we did not use the term 'counterfeit.'"[404] Asked later whether

---

[394] Email from Jackson Wetzel to Theotonius Rozario, Robert Kertesz et al. (March 31, 2011).
[395] *Ibid.*
[396] *Ibid.* The email also reminded Boeing that a component service bulletin (CSB) relating to the ice detection modules had already been released.
[397] Email from Jackson Wetzel to Theotonius Rozario and Robert Kertesz (July 27, 2011).
[398] Email from Robert Kertesz to Theotonius Rozario (July 27, 2011).
[399] Email from Theotonius Rozario to Robert Kertesz et al. (July 27, 2011).
[400] Email from Jeffrey Look to Thoetonius Rozario et al. (July 28, 2011).
[401] Email from Jackson Wetzel to Theotonius Rozario (July 28, 2011).
[402] *See* note 332, *supra.*
[403] Boeing, BOECOM messages TBC-KHS-11-0001-01B (August 31, 2011).
[404] Email from Scott Ecklund to Jackson Wetzel (August 18, 2011).

Boeing should have told its customers the parts were suspect counterfeit, Boeing's procurement agent said, "If we're going to be honest and open with the customers, yes."[405]

Boeing eventually replaced the suspect counterfeit part in the ice detection module in the P-8A. According to Boeing the reason for the replacement was to "ensure that customer concerns did not result in scheduling delays to the ongoing test flight."[406]

10. Reliability of Ice Detection Part

Almost as soon as the Xilinx FPGAs were identified as suspect counterfeit, BAE engineers concluded that the parts posed a reliability risk.[407] Boeing also concluded that the parts posed a reliability risk, stating in its June 2010 Suspect Discrepancy Report the components "may have somewhat lower reliability."[408] When later discussing the decision not to notify the Navy or its other customers about the suspect parts, however, Boeing's service engineer, said that "they were still good parts. Many used parts tend to have the same reliability as a new part."[409] He added that the Xilinx FPGAs in the ice detection modules were "used parts from a reputable and approved manufacturer."[410]

The Committee sent the manufacturer, Xilinx, a letter describing the anomalies that BAE had identified with the parts and asked the company about the reliability and performance risks of using FPGAs with those anomalies. Xilinx responded:

> Based on the description provided on the subject device, we would consider the devices to be of dubious origin. The devices may have been reclaimed and potentially exposed to excessive heat in order to dismount them from a circuit board. These cases pose a significant reliability risk owing to the potential exposure to excessive solder heat and electro-static discharge (ESD) damage. With respect to ESD, there are many potential damage mechanisms . . .. Some of these could be catastrophic; others may create a damage mechanism that is latent for an undetermined amount of time . . . The combination of these events calls into question the integrity of the devices and would have exposed them to potential ESD damage as well. Though the devices may initially function, it would be next to impossible to predict what amount of life is remaining, or what damage may have been caused to the circuitry.[411]

11. Suspect Counterfeit Parts in Other P-8A Systems

The FPGAs in ice detection modules were not the only suspect counterfeit electronic parts that ended up in a Navy P-8A. A second suspect counterfeit part, another Xilinx FPGA,

[405] Committee Staff interview of Theotonius Rozario (September 27, 2011) at 82.
[406] Boeing White Paper to the Senate Armed Services Committee (November 2011) at 1.
[407] Hall wrote, "Even though they are working, there is a reliability risk." Email from Murray Hall to Gary Hotchkin et al. (January 11, 2010).
[408] Boeing, *SDR Closure Template* (July 2010).
[409] Committee Staff interview of Robert Kertesz (September 30, 2011) at 52.
[410] *Ibid.*
[411] Letter from Moshe Gavielov to Honorable Carl Levin and John McCain (October 26, 2011).

was contained in Distance Measuring Equipment (DME) supplied by Honeywell to Boeing and installed in the Navy aircraft. In addition, suspect counterfeit electronic components supplied to Boeing by Rockwell Collins were also installed on P-8A aircraft.

a. Suspect Counterfeit Parts in P-8A Distance Measuring Equipment

According to Honeywell, Distance Measuring Equipment (DME) on the P-8A "provides continuous en route slant-range distance to select ground stations as well as for the non-precision approaches in terminal operations."[412] In 2008, Honeywell purchased thousands of Xilinx FPGAs for use in DME from two independent distributors, Serenity Electronics and Zelcon. Over 3,000 of the 5,500 Xilinx parts Honeywell purchased from Serenity were subsequently determined to have the incorrect die and Honeywell found that all the parts from both distributors showed evidence of remarking.[413] Honeywell also found that parts "show signs of delamination (separations in plastic packaging)" which Honeywell stated can lead to "increased failure rates over time."[414]

Boeing learned about the suspect counterfeit parts in DME in November 2010.[415] While Boeing requested a waiver from the Air Force in December 2010 to use the suspect counterfeit parts in DME installed on two C-17A aircraft that were about to be delivered, Boeing did not notify the Navy that five P-8A aircraft also contained suspect electronic parts in their DME.[416] In fact, Charles Dabundo, Boeing Defense Space and Security's (BDS) Program Manager for the P-8A, said that he only learned about the suspect counterfeit parts in the P-8A DME when he was preparing for his interview with Committee staff, nearly a year after Boeing had learned of the suspect parts from Honeywell.[417]

b. Additional Suspect Counterfeit Parts in P-8A

On July 7, 2010, Rockwell Collins notified Boeing of two suspect counterfeit parts used on Boeing programs. The parts had been supplied to Boeing by Rockwell Collins, which had purchased them from MVP Micro and Labra Electronics, two independent distributors whose operators were indicted in October 2009 for conspiracy, trafficking in counterfeit goods and mail fraud in connection with the importation of counterfeit electronic parts from China.[418]

---

[412] Honeywell International, *DME-37B Xilinx FPGA Suspect Parts Issue Boeing Applications* (November 30, 2010).
[413] *Ibid.* at 2.
[414] *Ibid.*
[415] Boeing answers to September 14, 2011 written questions from Committee Staff (October 21, 2011).
[416] Boeing, *Request for Deviation/Waiver* (December 8, 2010). The Air Force approved the waiver request for the C-17s on December 8, 2010, subject to corrective actions outlined in Boeing's request, including the retrofit by attrition of DME in already fielded aircraft that were affected by the suspect counterfeit part. The five P-8A aircraft containing DME with suspect counterfeit Xilinx FPGAs were YP001, YP003, YP004, YP006, and YP007. Boeing has said that the reason why a waiver was not sought from the Navy for the suspect counterfeit parts in the P-8A DME is because a waiver request happens at the time of final delivery to the government. The P-8A airplanes are test aircraft which, while they may reside at Patuxent River Naval Air Station and be flown by U.S. Navy pilots, have not been technically delivered to the government. Email from Benedict Cohen to Ilona Cohen et al. (August 19, 2011).
[417] Committee Staff interview of Charles Dabundo (November 8, 2011) at 30.
[418] United States Attorney's Office for the District of Columbia, *Press Release: Three California Family Members Indicted in Connection with Sales of Counterfeit High Tech Parts to the U.S. Military* (October 9, 2009).

On July 27, 2010, a Boeing quality assurance representative notified the Navy about the suspect counterfeit parts and indicated that they had been used on the P-8A.[419] Boeing subsequently tested samples of the parts to determine their authenticity. One sample was determined by Boeing to have been blacktopped and resurfaced. As to the second part, Boeing was unable to confirm who manufactured the part. In both cases, the company's recommendation was "to remove and replace" the parts.[420] Boeing removed the suspect counterfeit parts from two affected P-8A aircraft in November 2010 and February 2011, respectively.[421]

On April 4, 2012, Boeing notified the Committee of another suspect counterfeit part. According to the company, on May 14, 2010, "L3 Communications Systems notified BDS of suspect counterfeit Xilinx parts installed in two Digital Video Recorder units for the P-8A program."[422] Boeing stated that the suspect parts posed "no safety-of-flight issue" and that "affected units were captured by BDS and returned to L3 for rework within 90 days of the L3 notification, and prior to formal delivery of the affected aircraft."[423] The company, however, did not notify the Navy of the incident until March 27, 2012 – nearly two years after learning of the problem from L3.[424]

12. Boeing Process Impacts Counterfeits Reporting

As described above, the P-8A Poseidon is a derivative of a modified Boeing 737. According to Boeing, "In the past, commercial aircraft were sent to modification centers where they were taken apart and rebuilt to meet military specifications. The P-8A is Boeing's first military derivative aircraft to incorporate structural modifications to the aircraft as it moves through the commercial line."[425]

Boeing Commercial Airlines (BCA) and Boeing Defense, Space and Security (BDS) are separate divisions of the Boeing Company and each plays a role in the manufacture of the P-8A. BCA builds the airplanes to BDS's requirements and delivers them to BDS. BDS modifies the planes to meet the Navy's requirements.[426] Chuck Dabundo, BDS's P-8A Program Manager, described the relationship between Boeing Commercial and BDS as "analogous to a customer-supplier relationship."[427]

---

[419] Email from Alan Crowder to John Richardson (July 27, 2010).

[420] Boeing, *Analysis of Rockwell Collins Suspect Counterfeit Parts* (December 13, 2010).

[421] Email from Steve Koh to Joe Bryan (February 24, 2012).

[422] Email from Steve Koh to Joe Bryan (April 4, 2012).

[423] *Ibid.*

[424] Boeing told the Committee, "To improve visibility across all BDS programs of supplier notifications of escapement, including escapes of suspect counterfeit parts, BDS deployed a new, web-based application in January 2012. This new application provides a single source for documenting, managing, and tracking notifications of escapement." *Ibid.*

[425] Boeing Defense Space and Security Website, *available at* http://www.boeing.com/defense-space/military/p8a/index.html (February 24, 2012).

[426] Committee Staff interview of Charles Dabundo (November 8, 2011) at 3.

[427] *Ibid.* at 4-5. With respect to disposition of non-conforming parts on the P-8A, Boeing has said, "If nonconformances are encountered during the installation and checkout portion of the build that is executed by BDS, the processes utilized on the P-8A are governed by BDS's quality and material review processes, which are [Aerospace Standard] 9100 compliant, overseen by the Defense Contract Management Agency (DCMA), and part of

BDS and BCA each has its own process for addressing non-conformities like suspect counterfeit parts. While non-conformances identified by BDS or by a BDS supplier require review and corrective actions that include notification to the Cognizant Government Representative "within 24 hours of final disposition acceptance," the same requirement does not exist for nonconformities identified by BCA. [428] According to Mr. Dabundo, if a nonconformity is identified by BCA on a P-8A and BCA's recommendation is to use the nonconforming part (as was the case with the ice detection module), no notification to the Navy is required. [429]

According to a service engineer on the commercial side of Boeing, no one at Boeing ever advised him that BDS's contract with the Navy required notification. [430] In fact, the service engineer said that BDS is "treated like any other customer. We decide what notification the customers require or is deemed necessary." [431] As a result, BCA never even notified BDS that there was a suspect counterfeit Xilinx FPGA in the ice detection module. Mr. Dabundo, BDS's program manager for the P-8A, only found out about the suspect counterfeit part in the ice detection module around September 2011, well over a year and a half after Boeing became aware of it. Asked whether he was concerned that he was unaware of the issue for so long, Dabundo said, "No. I think, again, there are well-defined processes within BCA for dealing with these kinds of things." [432]

However, the Navy's contracts for the P-8A are with The Boeing Company, not BCA or BDS. [433] And those contracts include federal acquisition regulation 52.211-5 which states that "Used, reconditioned, or remanufacturer supplies . . . may be used in contract performance *if the contractor has proposed the use of such supplies, and the Contracting Officer has authorized their use.*" [434] In the case of the suspect counterfeit parts in the ice detection module, the U.S. Navy contracting officer for the P-8A was not even made aware of the issue for more than a year and a half after Boeing was informed of the problem.

While Boeing may believe that no notification to the Navy was required, the Navy disagrees. On October 31, 2011 the Navy's contracting officer wrote Boeing that "the Government's position is that any 'counterfeit' material received . . . is nonconforming material and shall be immediately reported to the Government." [435] Separately, the Navy has pointed out that Aerospace Standard 9100, a standard with which Boeing says it is compliant, states that non-conforming material – like the suspect counterfeit parts in the P-8As – shall not be used "unless

---

BDS's NAVAIR-approved P-8A Quality System in accordance with BDS's contract with the U.S. Navy." Boeing White Paper to the Senate Armed Services Committee (November 2011).

[428] Boeing Defense, Space & Security, *Material Review and Corrective Action System* (January 28, 2011); Committee Staff interview of Charles Dabundo (November 8, 2011) at 19.

[429] Committee Staff interview of Charles Dabundo (November 8, 2011) at 20, 36.

[430] Committee Staff interview of Robert Kertesz (September 30, 2011) at 16.

[431] *Ibid.*

[432] Committee Staff interview of Charles Dabundo (November 8, 2011) at 13. As discussed earlier, Dabundo only learned about the suspect counterfeit parts in the P-8A DME when he was preparing for his interview with Committee Staff which took place nearly a year after Boeing had learned of the parts. *Ibid.* at 30.

[433] Naval Air Systems Command Contract #N00019-09-C-0022 (April 13, 2009); Naval Air Systems Command Contract # N0019-04-C-3146-P00196 (June 29, 2004).

[434] Federal Acquisition Regulation 52.211-5 (August 2000) (emphasis added).

[435] Letter from Clare C. Carmack, Naval Air Systems Command, to Maureen Carlson (October 31, 2011).

specifically authorized by the customer if . . . the nonconformity results in a departure from the contract requirements."[436]

E. The Cost of Counterfeits - Counterfeit Electronic Parts in MDA THAAD Missiles

The cases above are just a few examples of the risks posed by counterfeit electronic parts. The Committee's investigation also uncovered dozens of other examples of suspect counterfeit electronic parts in military systems, including on thermal weapons sights delivered to the Army, on equipment that performs functional checks of military aircraft countermeasure dispenser systems, on telemetry boxes and missile interceptors used by the Missile Defense Agency (MDA), and on a wide range of military aircraft. In addition to the safety and national security risks they create, counterfeit electronic parts also drive up the cost of defense systems.

For example, counterfeit electronic parts pose long-term reliability problems, and reliability is a major driver in the overall cost of a weapon system. According to the Department of Defense's Director of Operational Test and Evaluation:

> Poor reliability is a problem with major implications for cost . . . Unreliable systems have higher sustainment costs because, quite plainly, they break more frequently than planned . . . Poor reliability leads to higher sustainment cost for replacement spares, maintenance, repair parts, facilities, staff, etc. Poor reliability hinders warfighter effectiveness and can essentially render weapons useless.[437]

Keeping down operations and sustainment costs is important, since they account for about two-thirds of the overall lifecycle costs of major weapons systems.[438]

Remediating counterfeit parts contained in military systems also drives up costs. To cite just one example, in September 2010, MDA learned that mission computers for THAAD missiles contained suspect counterfeit memory devices. According to MDA, if the devices had failed, the THAAD missile itself would likely have failed. The memory devices were purchased by Honeywell, a MDA subcontractor, from an independent electronic parts distributor. Honeywell installed the memory devices on mission computers which it then sold to Lockheed Martin. Lockheed, in turn, supplied the mission computers to MDA. While Honeywell and Lockheed notified MDA when they discovered the suspect parts, the nearly $2.7 million it cost to fix the problem was charged to the government. In January 2012, MDA reported that Lockheed Martin's award fee on the THAAD contract was later reduced by $2.1 million as a result of the suspect counterfeit parts in the mission computers.[439]

---

[436] Email from CAPT Don Martin to Joe Bryan (October 3, 2010). The Boeing facility that the P-8A is built in is certified to AS9100 Revision B.

[437] J. Michael Gilmore, Memorandum for Principal Deputy Under Secretary of Defense (Acquisition, Technology and Logistics, Subject: State of Reliability (June 30, 2010).

[438] *Ibid.*

[439] Missile Defense Agency Response to Senate Armed Services Committee Request for Information (January 31, 2012) at 2.

1. Honeywell Identifies Suspect Counterfeit Parts on THAAD Mission Computers

The Terminal High Altitude Area Defense (THAAD) system is an element of MDA's Ballistic Missile Defense System (BMDS) that provides "a globally transportable, rapidly deployable capability to intercept and destroy ballistic missiles . . .."[440] Lockheed Martin is MDA's prime contractor for THAAD fire units.[441] Honeywell manufactures THAAD mission computers as a subcontractor to Lockheed Martin.[442]

In September 2006, Honeywell purchased more than 1,700 Intel Flash memory devices from Hyper Technology, a Florida-based independent distributor of electronic parts. The flash devices were no longer in production and, according to Honeywell, were unavailable from the manufacturer.[443] The devices are used in dual processor module (DPM) circuit card assemblies (CCA) contained in THAAD mission computers. Each mission computer contains 16 Flash memory devices. The Flash devices in the DPM CCAs hold "critical software which provides vital instructions for the system processor to execute during missile flight to determine proper trajectory for target intercept[ion]."[444] According to MDA, the devices "are critical to maintain the functionality of the Mission Computer and ensure mission success" and a failure of the Flash memory devices would likely lead to a failure of the missile itself.[445]

A Honeywell investigation into the failure of a DPM CCA found that the lot date codes on Flash memory devices installed on the CCA "did not match their Configuration Management As-Built records."[446] That finding led Honeywell to examine other Flash memory devices in the company's inventory. In September 2010, Honeywell sent Flash devices pulled from its stock to a company lab for failure analysis. That analysis revealed evidence that the devices at issue were "used and refurbished." [447] Honeywell notified Lockheed Martin and MDA but by the time the problem was discovered, suspect counterfeit devices had already been installed and delivered in 50 THAAD mission computers.[448] In fact, MDA had actually flown one mission computer in a THAAD test flight.[449] Following the discovery of the counterfeit devices, Honeywell recommended recalling and reworking the 49 remaining mission computers to replace the

---

[440] Missile Defense Agency Website, *available at* http://www.mda.mil/system/thaad.html (last visited February 24, 2012).

[441] Lockheed Martin, *Press Release: Lockheed Martin Receives $619 Million Contract to Begin Production of THAAD Weapon System* (January 3, 2007).

[442] Lockheed Martin, *Press Release: Lockheed Martin's THAAD Missile Successful in Developmental Flight Test* (November 22, 2005).

[443] Honeywell International, *FUF Mission Computer TE 28 Flash Memory briefing to TPA and LMSSC* (October 4, 2010) at 5-13.

[444] Missile Defense Agency, *Information Brief* (October 17, 2011) at 6.

[445] *Ibid.*; Committee Staff Briefing with MDA (October 17, 2011).

[446] Honeywell International, *Honeywell Clearwater Anti-Counterfeit and Recall Manufacturing Readiness Assessment* (October 2010) at 1.

[447] Missile Defense Agency, *Information Brief* (October 17, 2011) at 13.

[448] *Ibid.* at 3. Honeywell documents indicate that mission computers were delivered between November 2008 and May 2010. Honeywell International, *FUF Mission Computer TE 28 Flash Memory Briefing to TPA and LMSSC* (October 4, 2010) at 9.

[449] Committee Staff briefing with MDA (October 17, 2011) at 3.

suspect devices.[450] Through October 2011, Honeywell had spent more than $1.94 million and Lockheed Martin had spent $675,000 to fix the problem.[451]

MDA attributed the failure to screen out the suspect counterfeits, in part, to "inadequate authenticity test requirements and lack of adherence to existing Honeywell internal inspection for [Electrical, Electronic, and Electromechanical] Parts procured from Brokers/Independent Distributors."[452] Honeywell itself pointed to "process gaps" and "detection opportunities missed" as contributing causes for its failure to identify the counterfeit devices prior to their use in the mission computers [453]

2. Lockheed and Honeywell Reimbursed for Fixing Mission Computers

MDA's contract with Lockheed Martin requires the government to reimburse the company for any reasonable costs incurred in the execution of the contract. While the root cause of the counterfeit Flash devices being installed on the mission computers was traced to failures by Honeywell, the nearly $2.7 million in costs associated with recalling the mission computers and removing and replacing the suspect devices were reimbursed by the government. MDA Director, Lieutenant General Patrick O'Reilly subsequently told the Committee, however, that those costs would be taken into account during MDA's process for determining the amount of Lockheed Martin's award fee under the THAAD contract.[454] In January 2012, MDA reported that Lockheed Martin's award fee was reduced by $2.1 million as a result of the suspect counterfeit parts in the mission computers.[455]

MDA's experience with suspect counterfeit electronic parts is not limited to the THAAD mission computers. LTG O'Reilly testified that, as of November 2011, "MDA and its contractors have suffered $4.5 million in rework costs due to counterfeit parts."[456] LTG O'Reilly has said, however, that the potential cost of remediating problems caused by counterfeit parts in defense systems could be much higher. He estimated, for example, that replacing suspect counterfeit parts in an operationally deployed MDA system "could cost hundreds of millions of dollars." [457]

---

[450] Honeywell International, *FUF Mission Computer TE 28 Flash Memory Briefing to TPA and LMSSC* (October 4, 2010) at 3.
[451] Lockheed Martin, *Honeywell Costs to Replace Suspect EEPROMs in MCs* (2011).
[452] Missile Defense Agency, *Information Brief* (October 17, 2011) at 3.
[453] Honeywell International, *FUF Mission Computer TE 28 Flash Memory Briefing to TPA and LMSSC* (October 4, 2010) at 14.
[454] SASC Hearing at 79.
[455] Missile Defense Agency Response to Senate Armed Services Committee Request for Information (January 31, 2012) at 2.
[456] SASC Hearing at 73.
[457] *Ibid.*

V.   Defense Logistics Agency

The examples discussed in Section IV involved suspect counterfeit parts that were integrated into new systems that were produced by defense contractors and sold to the military. The flood of counterfeit electronic parts in the defense supply chain also threatens the integrity of existing defense systems that depend on a steady stream of quality spare parts to keep them operating. The Defense Logistics Agency (DLA) is a Department of Defense combat support agency. DLA supplies more than 80 percent of the military's spare parts, including electronic parts.[458] DLA Land and Maritime manages the agency's supply chain for electronic parts.[459]

DLA identifies suspect counterfeit electronic parts by several means, including by reviewing Government Industry Data Exchange Program (GIDEP) reports[460] and Product Quality Deficiency Reports (PQDRs),[461] and through reports of suspect counterfeits received directly from the agency's customers and suppliers.[462] When the agency is alerted to a suspect part either by a customer or supplier or through a PQDR or GIDEP, DLA investigates to determine whether their inventory contains any of the suspect items. If suspect parts are identified in DLA inventory, they are designated as "non-issuable" and are tested by the agency's product testing center.[463]

In February 2011, the Committee requested that DLA provide a list of counterfeit electronic parts identified by or to the agency in either 2009 or 2010.[464] At that time, however, DLA did not maintain a list of cases in which the agency had identified actual or suspect counterfeit electronic parts.[465] To respond to the Committee's request, the agency's Product Testing Center reviewed more than 1,300 files associated with parts that had failed testing and provided the Committee with detailed information on cases where a part's failure was associated with it being suspect counterfeit.[466] At the time of the Committee's request, DLA did not have a uniform definition of counterfeit electronic part.[467] As a result, the Product Testing Center used

---

[458] DLA Website, *available at* http://www.dla.mil/Pages/ataglance.aspx (last visited February 22, 2012).

[459] Defense Logistics Agency, *Overview and Actions to Combat Counterfeit Parts* (December 16, 2010) at 5.

[460] GIDEP reports are filed by government agencies as well as private companies who do business with the government.

[461] PQDRs are filed by the military services "when they believe they have received a part which is not what they requested," including suspect counterfeits. DLA, *SASC Data Request concerning Suspect Counterfeit Electronics* (March 25, 2011) at 3.

[462] *Ibid.*

[463] *Ibid.*

[464] Email from Ilona Cohen to Robert Wimple et al. (February 18, 2011).

[465] Email from Robert Wimple to Ilona Cohen (March 3, 2011). Since the Committee's investigation, DLA has begun a monthly review of Product Test Center reports for parts determined to have characteristics of suspect counterfeits. Email from Cordell Francis to Joe Bryan (March 9, 2012).

[466] DLA, *SASC Data Request concerning Suspect Counterfeit Electronics* (May 11, 2011) at 1.

[467] According to GAO, as of early 2011, different DLA supply centers were operating with varying definitions of counterfeit with at least one DLA supply center defining parts as counterfeit only when they "misrepresented the part's trademark." GAO, *Defense Supplier Base Report: DOD Should Leverage Ongoing Initiatives in Developing Its Program to Mitigate Risk of Counterfeit Parts* (March 2010) at 4. DLA has since adopted the definition contained in Department of Defense Instruction 4140.01 issued on December 14, 2011, which defines "counterfeit material" as "material whose identity or characteristics have been deliberately misrepresented, falsified, or altered without legal right to do so." Answers to SASC Follow-On Questions (February 17, 2012) at 1; Department of Defense, *Instruction 4140.01: DOD Supply Chain Materiel Management Policy* (December 14, 2011) at 17.

the definition contained in the Committee's request in conducting its review.[468] The discussion in this section is limited to 202 cases identified by the Product Testing Center that involved either suspect integrated circuits or discrete devices, which were the focus of the Committee's investigation.[469]

A. *DLA List Includes Suppliers That Provided Suspect Parts on Multiple Occasions*

The 202 DLA-identified cases of suspect integrated circuits or discrete devices involved purchases from 93 separate companies. Thirty-seven of those companies provided suspect parts to DLA on more than one occasion. Of those 37, more than half provided suspect parts on three or more occasions. Ten suppliers provided suspect parts on five or more occasions and two companies provided suspect parts on more than 10 occasions.[470]

Only four of the 37 repeat suppliers of suspect parts identified by or to DLA in 2009 and 2010 were investigated by DLA "based on allegations regarding counterfeit parts."[471] The agency states that contractors that provide suspect counterfeit goods are supposed to be entered into an internal database called the Defense Contractors Review List (DCRL), which is "a repository for information related to a contractor's performance."[472] DLA personnel consult the DCRL to "determine if there is information on the DCRL that might have a bearing on the contractor's responsibility for the current award."[473] However, as of February 2012, only 36 of the 93 companies that supplied DLA suspect integrated circuits or discrete devices were on the DCRL. Some of those 36 were placed on the list more than a year after they supplied the suspect

---

[468] The Committee's request defined "suspect counterfeit" as a part that is suspected of: being an unauthorized copy; not conforming to the original component manufacturer (OCM) design, model, and/or performance standards; being "used" OCM product sold as "new"; having incorrect or false markings and/or documentation; or that was represented to be produced by an OCM, but was not in fact produced by that same OCM. DLA Land and Maritime Responses to SASC Request (February 10, 2012) at 6.

[469] DLA's review of testing files actually identified 381 suspect items from 135 suppliers. The agency deemed 130 items from 19 suppliers as "law enforcement sensitive" and did not provide detailed information on those items and their suppliers. Some of the 381 cases also involved electronic parts, such as rechargeable batteries and electron tubes, that are beyond the scope of the Committee's investigation. SASC Data Request Concerning Suspect Counterfeit Electronics (May 11, 2011) at 1.

[470] One of the two suppliers that provided suspect parts on more than ten occasions provided the majority under contracts with DLA that permitted the agency to test the product prior to their being accepted. However, nearly all of the remaining suspect parts were determined suspect after they had already been accepted. Defense Logistics Agency answers to February 18, 2011 written questions from Committee Staff (May 19, 2011).

[471] The investigations occurred in 2006, 2007, 2008, and 2011, respectively. DLA Land and Maritime Answers to SASC Follow-on Questions (February 17, 2012) at 1 DLA Land and Maritime Responses to SASC Request (February 10, 2012) at 2. DLA reported that 28 other companies on the list have been the subject of enforcement actions that were, in most cases, not "based upon or related to" the incidents the agency reported to the Committee.

[472] DLA Land and Maritime Responses to SASC Request (February 10, 2012) at 3; DLA Land and Maritime Answers to SASC Follow-on Questions (February 17, 2012) at 2.

[473] DLA Land and Maritime Responses to SASC Request (February 10, 2012) at 3.

parts.[474] Only 19 of the 37 companies identified as repeat suppliers of suspect parts were on the DCRL as of February 2012.[475]

In July 2011, DLA's Director issued a memorandum stating that "[c]onfirmed cases of counterfeit items shall be investigated and remedies obtained under existing fraud, waste, and abuse authorities."[476] As of March 2012, DLA was developing a revised policy and training for agency personnel on the use of the DCRL.[477]

B. Characteristics of DLA-Identified Suspect Counterfeit Parts

DLA provided the Committee with descriptions of failures that led its Product Testing Center to designate parts as suspect counterfeits. Among the reasons parts were deemed suspect were that they failed electrical tests;[478] showed signs of having been previously used, e.g., excess solder, scratches and bent leads;[479] were improperly marked and had date codes beyond the end-of-life production date;[480] and contained die with the wrong number.[481] Testing also found instances where commercial parts were substituted for parts that should have been military grade.[482]

As to their intended use, the suspect counterfeit parts identified by DLA were purchased to support hundreds of different weapons systems. In fact, DLA reported that 19 of the 202 parts are each used to support more than 100 different weapons systems. One part DLA identified as suspect is used in 176 different weapons systems.[483] Seventy-two of the parts are used in more than 25 weapons systems. Among the weapons systems that use parts DLA identified as suspect are B-52 bombers, CH-46 helicopters, F-15 Eagle, C-130 Hercules, Global Hawk, and the A-10 Thunderbolt aircraft. Twenty-six of the suspect counterfeit parts are used in nuclear reactor programs.[484]

---

[474] Defense Logistics Agency answers to February 18, 2011 written questions from Committee Staff (May 19, 2011). For example, one company identified in June 2010 by DLA as having provided suspect parts wasn't placed on the DCRL until December 2011. Defense Logistics Agency answers to February 24, 2012 written questions from Committee Staff (March 2, 2012).

[475] Defense Logistics Agency answers to February 24, 2012 written questions from Committee Staff (March 2, 2012).

[476] Vice Admiral A.S. Thompson Memorandum for DLA Executive Board, Subject: Supply Chain Management Policy for Counterfeit Items Prevention (July 21, 2011) at 1.

[477] Email from Gwendolyn Crimiel to Joe Bryan (March 2, 2012).

[478] See, e.g., DLA Product Testing Center, Request for and Results of Test – SPM7M207M8184 (January 12, 2009) at 2.

[479] See, e.g., DLA Product Testing Center, Request for and Results of Test – SP096002M3401 (May 10, 2010) at 2; DLA Product Testing Center, Request for and Results of Test – SPM7M510M3106 (May 24, 2010) at 2.

[480] See, e.g., DLA Product Testing Center, Request for and Results of Test – SP096005V2134 (January 8, 2010) at 2.

[481] See, e.g., DLA Product Testing Center, Request for and Results of Test – SP096006M3058 (September 29, 2010) at 3.

[482] See, e.g., DLA Product Testing Center, Request for and Results of Test – SP096003V1238 (January 27, 2009) at 1.

[483] Defense Logistics Agency answers to February 18, 2011 written questions from Committee Staff (May 19, 2011).

[484] Ibid.

C. DLA Rarely Filed GIDEP Reports

DLA uses information contained in Government-Industry Data Exchange Program (GIDEP) reports filed by government agencies and private companies to help the agency identify suspect parts in its own inventory.[485] DLA itself, however, rarely filed GIDEP reports for suspect parts it identified in 2009 and 2010. Of the 202 cases of suspect integrated circuits or discrete devices, only 15 were reported into GIDEP. Of those 15 reports, DLA itself filed only four. The remaining reports were filed by private companies or another DOD element.

In some cases, there may be ongoing criminal or other investigations that would warrant a delay in sharing information on a suspect part with the private companies who are members of GIDEP. However, in 2011, DLA provided the Committee with the names of all suppliers whose cases the agency considered "law enforcement sensitive." None of the 93 companies associated with the 202 cases was among them. In February 2012, DLA identified four companies from the list of 93 that have been investigated by the agency for supplying counterfeit parts.

DLA's practices with respect to GIDEP reporting have changed since the Committee's February 2011 request. A July 2011 Memorandum from DLA's Director, Vice Admiral A.S. Thompson stated that "Occurrences of suspect and confirmed counterfeit items shall be documented in the Government-Industry Data Exchange Program (GIDEP) as Agency Action Notices." [486] As of February 2012, DLA confirmed that its practice is to document "occurrences of suspect and confirmed counterfeit items in the Government-Industry Data Exchange Program (GIDEP) as Agency Action Notices."[487]

D. Suspect Counterfeit Parts in Federal Supply Classes 5961 and 5962

Notwithstanding shortcomings in investigating and reporting suspect counterfeits, DLA has taken steps to mitigate risk of acquiring some suspect parts. For example, DLA has identified semiconductor devices and microcircuits as two types of electronic parts that are at particular risk for counterfeiting.[488] In 2009, DLA established a "Qualified Suppliers List of Distributors" (QSLD) for semiconductor devices and microcircuits.[489] Among the requirements for distributors who wish to be included on the QSLD, are that they have a quality management system that meets DLA standards and that they purchase parts from the manufacturer or a distributor who itself is on the QSLD.[490] Distributors who wish to be included on the QSLD also undergo an audit that includes an "examination of applicable documents (including traceability records), processes and procedures, as well as the various systems required for attainment of

---

[485] DLA response to March 25, 2011 SASC data request concerning suspect counterfeit electronic parts (March 25, 2011) at 3.

[486] Vice Admiral A.S. Thompson Memorandum for DLA Executive Board, re: Supply Chain Management Policy for Counterfeit Items Prevention (July 21, 2011) at 5.

[487] DLA, *Proposed Answers to SASC Follow-On Questions* (February 10, 2012) at 1.

[488] Those two types of parts fall under Federal Stock Classes (FSC) 5961 and 5962, respectively. DLA, *Criteria and Provisions for Qualified Suppliers List of Distributors, DSCC-QSLD-5961/5962 A (QSLD)* (April 8, 2009) at 2.

[489] *Ibid.*

[490] *Ibid.* at 5.

qualification."[491] DLA may conduct random audits of distributors after they are approved for the QSLD.[492]

QSLDs have a preferred status in DLA solicitations for semiconductor devices and microcircuits. DLA described the process for determining who receives an award for those parts:

> Awards are made to the suppliers based on a number of factors including the risk associated with the parts, particularly in these FSCs. The least risk is associated with an Approved Source (per the drawing or catalog information) followed by the Qualified Manufacturers List or Qualified Parts List source. If the part is not available from one of these sources, the next most favorable source is a QSLD supplier with traceability. If the QSLD supplier does not have traceability on the items, they are considered as any other supplier would be. The next most-favorable would be a supplier with acceptable traceability that is provided and examined prior to award of the contract.[493]

While the purpose of the QSLD is to mitigate risk, the success of the program is dependent on QSLD companies actually supplying parts to DLA. As of February 2012 there were only 26 companies on the QSLD and DLA often purchases semiconductor devices and microcircuits from distributors who are not on the QSLD.[494] In fact, in Fiscal Year 2011, DLA issued just over more than 3,600 awards for semiconductor devices and microcircuits. Only 52 percent of the awards were issued to companies on the QSLD.[495]

---

[491] *Ibid.* at 7; DLA Land and Maritime Responses to SASC Request (February 10, 2012) at 1.

[492] DLA, *Criteria and Provisions for Qualified Suppliers List of Distributors, DSCC-QSLD-5961/5962 A (QSLD)* (April 8, 2009) at 7.

[493] DLA Land and Maritime Responses to SASC Request (February 10, 2012) at 1.

[494] Defense Logistics Agency, *Qualified Suppliers List of Distributors* (February 9, 2012).

[495] DLA Land and Maritime Responses to SASC Request (February 10, 2012) at 1.

VI.   SASC Legislation Targets Counterfeit Electronic Parts

On November 8, 2011, the Senate Armed Services Committee held a hearing to explore the problem of counterfeit electronic parts infiltrating critical defense systems and the risk those parts pose to such systems. The hearing also examined steps necessary to mitigate that risk and actions taken by defense contractors upon discovery that counterfeit electronic parts have been integrated into weapons systems.

Following that hearing, Committee Chairman Carl Levin and Ranking Member John McCain offered an amendment to the FY 2012 National Defense Authorization Act to address weaknesses in the defense supply chain identified through the Committee's investigation and to promote the adoption of aggressive counterfeit avoidance practices by DOD and the defense industry. The amendment was adopted in the Senate and a revised version was included in the final bill signed by President Barack Obama on December 31, 2011. In addition to requiring the Secretary to issue regulations defining the term "counterfeit" for DOD,[496] the law seeks to:

- Prevent counterfeit electronic parts from entering the U.S. supply chain by enhancing the inspection regime for imported electronic parts and authorizing government officials to share information with manufacturers to identify counterfeits;

- Reduce the risk of acquiring counterfeit parts by ensuring parts are bought, whenever possible, from manufacturers, authorized distributors, and trusted suppliers;

- Stop counterfeit parts before they are integrated into defense systems by requiring DOD and the defense industry to establish policies and procedures to inspect and test electronic parts;

- Improve transparency by mandating the written notification of counterfeit electronic parts to the government; and,

- Strengthen the incentive to avoid and detect counterfeit electronic parts by ensuring that the cost of replacing suspect parts is paid by contractors, not the government.

Several of the law's requirements are in line with the Society of Automotive Engineers (SAE) Aerospace Standard 5553 (AS5553) *Counterfeit Electronic Parts: Avoidance, Detection, Mitigation and Disposition Policy*. Released in April 2009, AS5553 is a product of a joint government-industry committee established by SAE to "to address aspects of preventing, detecting, responding to and counteracting the threat of counterfeit electronic components."[497] A

---

[496] On December 14, 2011, while the 2012 NDAA conference report was being debated in the Congress, DOD issued Department of Defense Instruction ("DODI") 4140.01 DOD Supply Chain Materiel Management Policy. The DODI defined "counterfeit materiel" as materiel whose identity or characteristics have been deliberately misrepresented, falsified, or altered without the legal right to do so." Department of Defense, *Instruction 4140.01: DOD Supply Chain Materiel Management Policy* (December 14, 2011) at 17.

[497] SAE International, Presentation on SAE Standards on Counterfeit Avoidance and Mitigation (July 29, 2011) at 1 (hereinafter "July 29, 2011 SAE Presentation"). Among defense industry members were Boeing, General Dynamics, L-3, Lockheed Martin, Northrop Grumman, and Raytheon. Government members included the Defense Logistics Agency (DLA), Defense Contract Management Agency (DCMA), Federal Aviation Administration

number of defense contractors have endorsed AS5553 and it was adopted by the Department of Defense in August 2009.[498]

A. *Keeping Counterfeit Parts Out of the Supply Chain*

The Committee's investigation identified approximately 1,800 cases of suspect counterfeit parts in the defense supply chain. Eighty percent of the first tier suppliers of those parts were based in the United States. However, the evidence suggests that the overwhelming majority of those suspect parts did not originate in the United States. It is therefore critical that the United States stop counterfeit electronic parts before they enter the country. The 2012 NDAA contains two provisions directed at that goal. The first strengthens the inspection regime for imported electronic parts. The second ensures that the government can seek appropriate assistance from the private sector in determining whether an imported product is authentic.

With respect to border inspections, the law requires the Secretary of Homeland Security to consult with the Secretary of Defense on the source countries for counterfeit electronic parts in the defense supply chain and to implement a program of enhanced inspection of imported electronic parts. An effective system for inspecting imports depends, however, on the ability of government inspectors to distinguish authentic from counterfeit products. Methods used by electronic parts counterfeiters are making that increasingly difficult.

One way to improve the government's ability to determine whether imported parts are authentic is to enlist the assistance of electronic part manufacturers. Manufacturers have expressed a willingness to provide such assistance and have said that it was once the government's practice to share with them samples or pictures of suspect counterfeit goods stopped at the border to help determine their authenticity.[499] Notwithstanding past practices, U.S. Customs and Border Protection (CBP) told the Committee in 2011 that the Trade Secrets Act "prohibits the disclosure prior to seizure of confidential business information found on merchandise suspected of [being counterfeit]."[500]

The 2012 NDAA remedies that by explicitly authorizing the Secretary of the Treasury to share information from and samples of suspect products, their packaging and labels with the company whose product is suspected of being counterfeited.

(FAA), U.S. Navy, Naval Air Warfare Center, U.S. Missile Defense Agency (MDA), and NASA. July 29, 2011 SAE Presentation at 2-3.

[498] Department of Defense, *Adoption Notice for SAE AS5553, "Counterfeit Electronic Parts; Avoidance, Detection, Mitigation, and Disposition* (August 2009); Committee Staff interview of Vivek Kamath (October 6, 2011) at 33; Letter from Tim Keating, Boeing, to Senators Carl Levin and John McCain (November 8, 2011).

[499] SASC Hearing at 44.

[500] According to the CBP, "product identity information, such as serial numbers, dates of manufacture, lot codes, batch numbers, and universal product codes, found on the surface of detained trademarked merchandise or its packaging (or, in the case of digital information, embedded in semiconductors inside the merchandise) constitutes confidential business information." Letter from The Honorable Alan D. Bersin to Senator Carl Levin (December 6, 2011) at 1.

B. Reducing Supplier-Related Risks

As described above, the defense industry's waning influence in the semiconductor market and the shrinking production lifecycle of electronic parts have combined to make defense systems increasingly vulnerable to electronic part obsolescence. Faced with the loss of trusted, stable sources of supply for certain electronic parts, DOD and defense companies often turn to independent distributors. However, the risk of obtaining counterfeit parts in the independent distribution market is significantly higher than from the manufacturer or authorized distributor.

One way to mitigate the risk of obtaining counterfeit parts from independent distributors is to audit potential distributors and develop a list of trusted suppliers.[501] The Missile Defense Agency (MDA) performs site assessments of independent distributors and audits past performance in determining whether to approve them as a source of electronic parts.[502] The results of MDA's assessments, to date, demonstrate why that practice is so critical.

As of November 2011, MDA had conducted inspections of 51 independent distributors. According to LTG O'Reilly, "more than 60 percent [of those 51 independent distributors] were assessed as moderate to high risk for providing counterfeit products."[503] MDA found independent distributors that engaged in "deceptive marketing" by posting photos of fake facilities on their website to appear more established or to misrepresent the size of their operations.[504] One independent distributor even listed its address as a corporate building when the actual "facility" was located at a local United Parcel Service store.[505]

The FY 2012 NDAA includes provisions aimed at eliminating DOD and defense industry purchases of electronic parts from unknown or suspect suppliers. The law requires the Secretary of Defense to promulgate regulations mandating that, whenever possible, DOD, defense contractors, and subcontractors purchase electronic parts that are in production or available in stock from the manufacturers or their authorized distributors. As discussed above, 30 percent of the suspect counterfeit parts identified by the Committee, for which information was available, were in production as of May 2011. Independent distributors were the source of almost all of those parts. Requiring DOD and contractors to purchase electronic parts that are in production, whenever possible, from manufacturers or their authorized distributors should significantly reduce that percentage going forward.

For parts that are out of production or not readily available in stock, the FY 2012 NDAA requires the Secretary to issue regulations requiring DOD, defense contractors and subcontractors to buy from "trusted suppliers." DOD is responsible for establishing qualification requirements for trusted suppliers that ensure they have appropriate policies and procedures in place to detect and avoid counterfeit electronic parts. While the regulations will permit contractors to use trusted suppliers other than those identified by the Department, contractors

---

[501] *See, e.g.*, Committee Staff interview of Vivek Kamath (October 6, 2011) at 28, 33-34; SASC Hearingat 73-75.
[502] SASC Hearing at 73-75.
[503] *Ibid.* at 73.
[504] MDA, *MDA Information Briefing to the Senate Armed Services Committee on Counterfeit Parts* (December 15, 2010) at 4.
[505] *Ibid.*

must comply with established industry standards in identifying their own trusted suppliers. AS5553, which is the primary industry standard relating to counterfeit electronic parts, requires companies to assess sources of supply to determine the risk of obtaining counterfeit parts and lists a number of possible assessment actions to review a potential supplier's performance.[506] Regulations issued pursuant to the FY 2012 NDAA will also provide DOD the right to review and audit the selection of trusted suppliers.

C. Stopping Counterfeit Parts Through Testing

According to the Semiconductor Industry Association (SIA) "sophisticated equipment and advanced labeling techniques [are] making it increasingly difficult to identify fake semiconductors."[507] That view is echoed by companies in the defense industry. As L-3's Vice-President for Procurement put it, "[Counterfeiters] are not dumb people. They know how to do counterfeiting. They know how counterfeiting is being detected. And they come up with ways of beating the detection systems."[508]

Companies that conduct authenticity testing have also lamented the difficulty of keeping pace with the counterfeiters. Thomas Sharpe, the president of an independent distributor and testing lab, told the Committee that "counterfeiters are most certainly monitoring our level of detection expertise and quickly evolving newer processes to introduce into the global supply chains. Many of the current counterfeit[ing] techniques are already beyond the in-house detection capabilities of most open-market suppliers."[509] While eliminating counterfeit electronic parts from the supply chain will continue to pose a challenge, aggressive inspection and testing practices can reduce the number and impact of counterfeit parts that make it through.

The Committee's investigation identified wide disparities in testing protocols used by DLA and companies in the defense supply chain. Some require a range of testing to determine authenticity before they are willing to accept parts, while others are willing to accept parts that have only been subject to basic testing. In an example of the risks associated with the latter, the suspect counterfeit transistors that were integrated into Bus Adaptor Units on the U.S. Air Force's C-27J, described in Section IV above, passed basic electrical testing that was only designed to "ensure functionality."[510] However, subsequent, more comprehensive testing of transistors from the same date code and supplier found three different types of die in four transistors that were analyzed and product markings that actually wiped off the parts, leading the tester to conclude the parts were counterfeit.[511]

The process used to determine whether parts are subject to testing at all can also affect the risk of purchasing counterfeit parts. For example, a recent Department of Justice filing in a case involving counterfeit electronic parts, described a scheme whereby prospective buyers

---

[506] AS5553 at 5.

[507] SASC Hearing at 36.

[508] Committee Staff interview of Ralph DeNino (October 24, 2011) at 10.

[509] SASC Hearing at 25.

[510] *See* Section IV, *infra*; New Advantage Purchase Order N. 264450 to White Horse (January 13, 2009).

[511] Anloy Technologies, *Product Analysis Report N. ATI1625* (February 19, 2009) at 1.

"were sent legitimate sample devices, which passed buyer testing, but orders were fulfilled with counterfeit goods."[512]

As AS5553 states, inspection and testing "may not definitively distinguish authentic parts from counterfeit parts" but they can "minimize the risk of counterfeit parts entering the production system."[513] The FY 2012 NDAA requires the Secretary of Defense to conduct an assessment and issue guidance on DOD acquisition policies and systems for the detection and avoidance of counterfeit electronic parts. The law also requires the Secretary to implement a program requiring contractors to establish policies and procedures to address inspection and testing.

D. *Mitigating Risk through Reporting and Notification*

The Committee's investigation uncovered several cases in which defense contractors failed to inform DOD about suspect counterfeit electronic parts they had identified in defense systems delivered to the U.S. military. To cite just one example, in January 2010, BAE informed Boeing that ice detection modules BAE had sold the company contained suspect parts. Boeing subsequently installed one of those modules on a Navy P-8A Poseidon airplane. However, the company only informed the Navy about the suspect part in August 2011. And that notification only came after the Committee made multiple inquiries to Boeing.

Failing to notify the military that a defense system contains a suspect counterfeit part can risk the performance of that system and the safety of military personnel who rely on it. The FY 2012 NDAA contains provisions to prevent that from happening. The law requires the Secretary of Defense to issue regulations mandating that DOD and department contractors notify appropriate government authorities in writing within 60 days of becoming aware of, or having reason to suspect, that items purchased by or for DOD contain counterfeit electronic part.

As discussed above, the Government Industry Data Exchange Program (GIDEP) is a DOD-run system that provides a forum for industry and government to report suspect counterfeit parts and the suppliers who sold them. GIDEP reports are available online for review by program participants and include information on the part numbers for counterfeits that have been found, methods used by counterfeiters, and suppliers who provided suspect parts. Raytheon's Vice President of Supply Chain Operations said that information in GIDEP:

> [A]llows us to be proactive in knowing when there are known threats and allows us to make sure that if I know there is a chip or a transistor that is counterfeit, that my competitors in industry are not going and buying at the same time and I already know it's a counterfeit. We can stop them from doing it . . . we use the GIDEP to share information, warn each other of something that is a real threat, so some other company does not go off and buy parts from that supplier or those parts in particular.

---

[512] McCloskey Sentencing Memorandum at 29.
[513] AS5553 at 21.

The number of reports filed in GIDEP, however, is a small fraction of the total number of suspect counterfeits. As discussed above, while the Committee's review identified approximately 1,800 cases of suspect counterfeit electronic parts in the defense supply chain in 2009 and 2010, only 271 reports of suspect counterfeits were filed in GIDEP during that same period. The 2012 NDAA sought to remedy that by requiring DOD personnel and contractors to report suspect counterfeit parts to GIDEP or a similar program designated by the Secretary of Defense.

On December 14, 2011, as the 2012 NDAA conference report was being debated in the Congress, DOD issued a Department of Defense Instruction (DODI) stating that "all occurrences of suspect and confirmed counterfeit items will be documented in the appropriate reporting system to include the GIDEP."[514] The DODI also directed DOD's Director of Defense Procurement and Acquisition Policy to "develop procurement instructions and procedures . . . including appropriate contract language and reporting requirements to GIDEP and law enforcement agencies."[515]

E. Strengthening Contractor Incentives for Avoiding and Detecting Counterfeit Parts

In September 2010, MDA learned that mission computers for THAAD missiles supplied by Lockheed Martin contained suspect counterfeit memory devices. As discussed above, the memory devices had been purchased by Honeywell and installed on mission computers which the company sold to Lockheed Martin. Despite Honeywell's own finding that "process gaps" and "detection opportunities missed" contributed to its failure to identify the counterfeit devices, Honeywell and Lockheed Martin were reimbursed the nearly $2.7 million it cost the two companies to fix the mission computers.[516] (In January 2012, MDA reported that Lockheed Martin's award fee on the THAAD contract was later reduced by $2.1 million as a result of the suspect counterfeit parts in the mission computers.[517])

Permitting contractors to recover costs incurred as a result of their own failure to detect counterfeit electronic parts does not encourage their adoption of aggressive counterfeit avoidance and detection programs. Government contracts that permit cost recovery in such circumstances also contrast with agreements contractors enter with their own suppliers. For example, Raytheon's General Terms and Conditions relating to nonconforming material state that the "[c]ost of repair, rework, replacement, inspection, transportation, repackaging, and/or reinspection by Buyer shall be at Seller's expense."[518] Similarly, BAE's General Provisions state that, in cases where a supplier delivers non-conforming work, BAE may "make, or have a

---

[514] Department of Defense, *Instruction 4140.01: DOD Supply Chain Materiel Management Policy* (December 14, 2011) at 13.
[515] *Ibid.* at 8.
[516] Lockheed Martin, *Honeywell Costs to Replace Suspect EEPROMs in MCs* (2011); Honeywell International, *FUF Mission Computer TE 28 Flash Memory Briefing to TPA and LMSSC* (October 4, 2010) at 14.
[517] Missile Defense Agency Response to Senate Armed Services Committee Request for Information (January 31, 2012) at 2.
[518] Raytheon, *General Terms and Conditions of Purchase* (undated) at 3.

third party make all repairs, modifications, or replacements necessary to enable work to comply in all respects with Contract requirements and charge the cost incurred to the SELLER."[519]

The 2012 NDAA requires the Secretary of Defense to issue regulations requiring that costs associated with remediating the use of counterfeit or suspect counterfeit parts in defense systems are paid by contractors who supplied them rather than the government. Those regulations will strengthen incentives for contractor adoption of aggressive counterfeit avoidance and detection programs and align DOD contracts with best practices in the commercial sector.

On March 16, 2012, the Acting Undersecretary of Defense for Acquisition, Technology and Logistics (AT&L) issued counterfeit prevention guidance to military departments and defense agencies directing "specific actions to prevent, detect, remediate, and investigate counterfeiting in the DoD supply chain."[520] Among the specific actions directed by AT&L are that DOD Components establish testing and verification requirements for certain acquisitions from sources other than original manufacturers or their authorized distributors; that DOD Components, their contractors and subcontractors report suspect parts to GIDEP; and that Components develop and provide training for DOD personnel on addressing the counterfeit problem.[521]

---

[519] BAE Systems, *General Provisions Commercial Subcontracts/Purchase Orders* (undated) at 5 (emphasis in original).
[520] Undersecretary of Defense for Acquisition, Technology and Logistics, *Memorandum for Secretaries of the Military Departments, Directors of the Defense Agencies* (March 16, 2012).
[521] *Ibid.*

COMMITTEE ACTION

On May 15, 2012, by voice vote, the Committee adopted the report and conclusions of the inquiry into counterfeit electronic parts in the Department of Defense supply chain. Twenty-two Senators were present. No Senator voted in the negative.

APPENDIX

United States Government Accountability Office

GAO

Report to the Committee on Armed
Services, U.S. Senate

February 2012

DOD SUPPLY CHAIN

Suspect Counterfeit Electronic Parts Can Be Found on Internet Purchasing Platforms

G A O
Accountability * Integrity * Reliability

GAO-12-375

February 2012

DOD SUPPLY CHAIN

Suspect Counterfeit Electronic Parts Can Be Found on Internet Purchasing Platforms

Why GAO Did This Study

Counterfeit parts—generally the misrepresentation of parts' identity or pedigree—can seriously disrupt the Department of Defense (DOD) supply chain, harm weapon systems integrity, and endanger troops' lives. In a November testimony (GAO-12-213T), GAO summarized preliminary observations from its investigation into the purchase and authenticity testing of selected, military-grade electronic parts that may enter the DOD supply chain. As requested, this report presents GAO's final findings on this issue. The results are based on a nongeneralizable sample and cannot be used to make inferences about the extent to which parts are being counterfeited.

GAO created a fictitious company and gained membership to two Internet platforms providing access to vendors selling military-grade electronic parts. GAO requested quotes from numerous vendors to purchase a total of 16 parts from three categories: (1) authentic part numbers for obsolete and rare parts; (2) authentic part numbers with postproduction date codes (date codes after the last date the part was manufactured); and (3) bogus, or fictitious, part numbers that are not associated with any authentic parts. To determine whether the parts received were counterfeit, GAO contracted with a qualified, independent testing lab for full component authentication analysis of the first two categories of parts, but not the third (bogus) category. Part numbers have been altered for reporting purposes.

GAO is not making recommendations in this report.

View GAO-12-375. For more information, contact Richard J. Hillman at (202) 512-6722 or hillmanr@gao.gov or Timothy Persons at (202) 512-6522 or personst@gao.gov.

What GAO Found

Suspect counterfeit and bogus—part numbers that are not associated with any authentic parts—military-grade electronic parts can be found on Internet purchasing platforms, as none of the 16 parts vendors provided to GAO were legitimate. "Suspect counterfeit," which applies to the first two categories of parts that were tested, is the strongest term used by an independent testing lab, signifying a potential violation of intellectual property rights, copyrights, or trademark laws, or misrepresentation to defraud or deceive. After submitting requests for quotes on both platforms, GAO received responses from 396 vendors, of which 334 were located in China; 25 in the United States; and 37 in other countries, including the United Kingdom and Japan. Of the 16 parts purchased, vendors usually responded within a day. GAO selected the first of any vendor among those offering the lowest prices that provided enough information to purchase a given part, generally within 2 weeks. Under GAO's selection methodology, all 16 parts were provided by vendors in China.

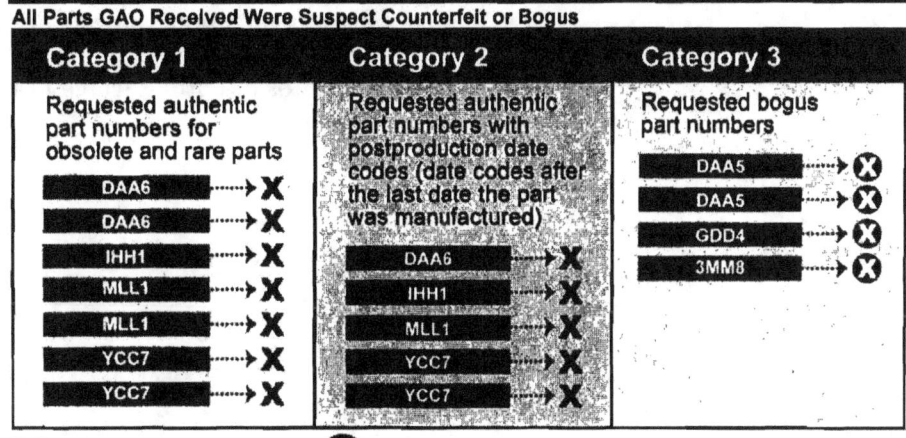

All Parts GAO Received Were Suspect Counterfeit or Bogus

Category 1	Category 2	Category 3
Requested authentic part numbers for obsolete and rare parts	Requested authentic part numbers with postproduction date codes (date codes after the last date the part was manufactured)	Requested bogus part numbers
DAA6 → X		DAA5 → Ⓧ
DAA6 → X		DAA5 → Ⓧ
IHH1 → X	DAA6 → X	GDD4 → Ⓧ
MLL1 → X	IHH1 → X	3MM8 → Ⓧ
MLL1 → X	MLL1 → X	
YCC7 → X	YCC7 → X	
YCC7 → X	YCC7 → X	

X - Suspect counterfeit part   **Ⓧ** - Bogus part

Source: GAO analysis of independent laboratory test results.

Note: Part numbers shown have been altered from the part numbers used for purchasing.

Specifically, all 12 of the parts received after GAO requested rare part numbers or postproduction date codes were suspect counterfeit, according to the testing lab. Multiple authentication tests, ranging from inspection with electron microscopes to X-ray analysis, revealed that the parts had been re-marked to display the part numbers and manufacturer logos of authentic parts. Other features were found to be deficient from military standards, such as the metallic composition of certain pieces. For the parts requested using postproduction date codes, the vendors also altered date markings to represent the parts as newer than when they were last manufactured, as verified by the parts' makers. Finally, after submitting requests for bogus parts using invalid part numbers, GAO purchased four parts from four vendors, which shows their willingness to supply parts that do not technically exist.

_____ **United States Government Accountability Office**

Contents

Abbreviations

DLA	Defense Logistics Agency
DOD	Department of Defense
RTS	resistance to solvents
SEM	scanning electron microscopy
XRF	X-ray florescence

G A O
Accountability * Integrity * Reliability

United States Government Accountability Office
Washington, DC 20548

February 21, 2012

The Honorable Carl Levin
Chairman
The Honorable John McCain
Ranking Member
Committee on Armed Services
United States Senate

Counterfeit parts—generally the misrepresentation of parts' identity or pedigree—have the potential to seriously disrupt the Department of Defense (DOD) supply chain, delay missions, affect the integrity of weapon systems, and ultimately endanger the lives of our troops. Almost anything is at risk of being counterfeited, from fasteners used on aircraft to electronics used on missile guidance systems. There can be many sources of counterfeit parts as DOD draws from a large network of global suppliers.[1]

In 2011, we reported that the increase in counterfeit electronic parts is one of several potential barriers DOD faces in addressing parts quality problems.[2] More recently, you asked about the availability of counterfeit parts on Internet platforms commonly used to buy hard-to-find military-grade electronic parts, including those used in weapon systems. In a November testimony, we summarized preliminary observations from our investigation into the purchase and authenticity testing of selected, military-grade electronic parts that may enter the DOD supply chain.[3] This report presents our final findings on this issue.

In conducting this investigation, we created a fictitious company to gain access to Internet platforms that provide access to vendors selling

---

[1] GAO, *Defense Supplier Base: DOD Should Leverage Ongoing Initiatives in Developing Its Program to Mitigate Risk of Counterfeit Parts*, GAO-10-389 (Washington, D.C.: Mar. 29, 2010).

[2] GAO, *Space and Missile Defense Acquisitions: Periodic Assessment Needed to Correct Parts Quality Problems in Major Programs*, GAO-11-404 (Washington, D.C.: June 24, 2011).

[3] GAO, *DOD Supply Chain: Preliminary Observations Indicate That Counterfeit Electronic Parts Can Be Found on Internet Purchasing Platforms*, GAO-12-213T (Washington, D.C.: Nov. 8, 2011).

military-grade electronic parts. Our company included a fictitious owner and employees, mailing and e-mail addresses, a website, and a listing on the Central Contractor Registration.[4] We attempted to purchase memberships to three Internet platforms that were of interest to this committee. One platform granted us membership despite not receiving all requested supporting documentation, the second granted us membership after we supplied the requested documentation as well as fictitious business references, and the third denied our request for membership even after we provided all documentation and references. None of the platforms contacted our references. We then requested quotes from vendors on both platforms to purchase a total of 16 parts from three categories: (1) authentic part numbers for obsolete and rare parts; (2) authentic part numbers with postproduction date codes (date codes after the last date the part was manufactured); and (3) bogus, or fictitious, part numbers that are not associated with any authentic parts. Using a list of four authentic part numbers this committee provided, we purchased 7 parts from the first category and 5 parts from the second (for which we altered only the date code). We independently verified with the Defense Logistics Agency (DLA) that these part numbers were used for military applications using DLA's Federal Logistics Information System and by interviewing DLA officials.[5] We used three invalid part numbers provided by the committee, which altered portions of existing part numbers that identify certain performance specifications, to purchase the 4 bogus parts. We then confirmed with DLA and selected part manufacturers that the numbers we developed were invalid. We altered all part numbers for reporting purposes.

We requested parts from vendors that were new in original packaging, not refurbished, and had no mixed date codes. We selected the first vendor among those offering the lowest prices that provided enough information, such as name, addresses, and payment method, to make a purchase. We attempted to avoid using the same vendor more than once unless no other vendor responded to our request; however, vendors may operate under more than one name. We did not attempt to verify the

---

[4] The Central Contractor Registration is the primary contractor registrant database for the U.S. federal government. The Central Contractor Registration collects, validates, stores, and disseminates data in support of agency acquisition missions.

[5] DLA's Federal Logistics Information System via the World Wide Web provides general information about more than 8 million supply items used by the U.S. government and North Atlantic Treaty Organization (NATO) allies.

independence of any vendor before we made our purchases. Finally, we contracted with the SMT Corp. for full component authentication analysis.[6] For details on this analysis, see appendix I.

The results of this investigation are based on the use of a nongeneralizable sample, and these results cannot be used to make inferences about the extent to which parts are being counterfeited. We conducted this investigation from August 2011 to February 2012 in accordance with standards prescribed by the Council of the Inspectors General on Integrity and Efficiency.

Suspect Counterfeit Electronic Parts Can Be Found on Internet Purchasing Platforms

As shown in figure 1, each of the 16 parts we purchased was either suspect counterfeit or bogus. Specifically, all 12 of the parts we received after requesting authentic part numbers (either with valid or invalid date codes) were suspect counterfeit, according to SMT Corp. In addition, vendors provided us with 4 bogus parts after we requested invalid part numbers, which demonstrates their willingness to sell parts that do not technically exist. The following sections detail our findings for each of the three categories of parts we purchased.

Under our selection methodology, the 16 parts we purchased were provided by 13 vendors in China. After submitting requests for quotes on both platforms, we received responses from 396 vendors, of which 334 were located in China; 25 in the United States; and 37 in other countries, including the United Kingdom and Japan. All 40 of the responses we received for the bogus part numbers were from vendors located in China (6 of these vendors also offered to sell us parts for the authentic part numbers we requested). We selected the first of any vendor among those offering the lowest prices that provided enough information to purchase a given part, generally within 2 weeks.[7] As such, 3 vendors each supplied 2 parts and 10 vendors each supplied 1 part. We sent 13 payments to Shenzhen, 2 payments to Shantou, and 1 payment to Beijing. Despite operating under different company names, 2 vendors provided us with

---

[6] We selected SMT Corp. as the independent, full component authentication testing laboratory based on its (1) ability to conduct 100 percent component inspection with transmission X-rays, (2) use of a patented heated solvent test, and (3) use of scanning electron microscopy to detect surface abnormalities as well as doing spectroscopic analysis of surface material on the components.

[7] These vendors usually responded to our initial requests for quotes within a day.

identical information for sending payment (name of representative and contact information). There could be a number of explanations for this, ranging from legitimate (the vendors handle payments through the same banker or accountant) to potentially deceptive (same individuals representing themselves as multiple companies). Thirteen parts were then shipped from Shenzhen and 3 from Hong Kong.

Figure 1: Status of Parts Purchased and Tested

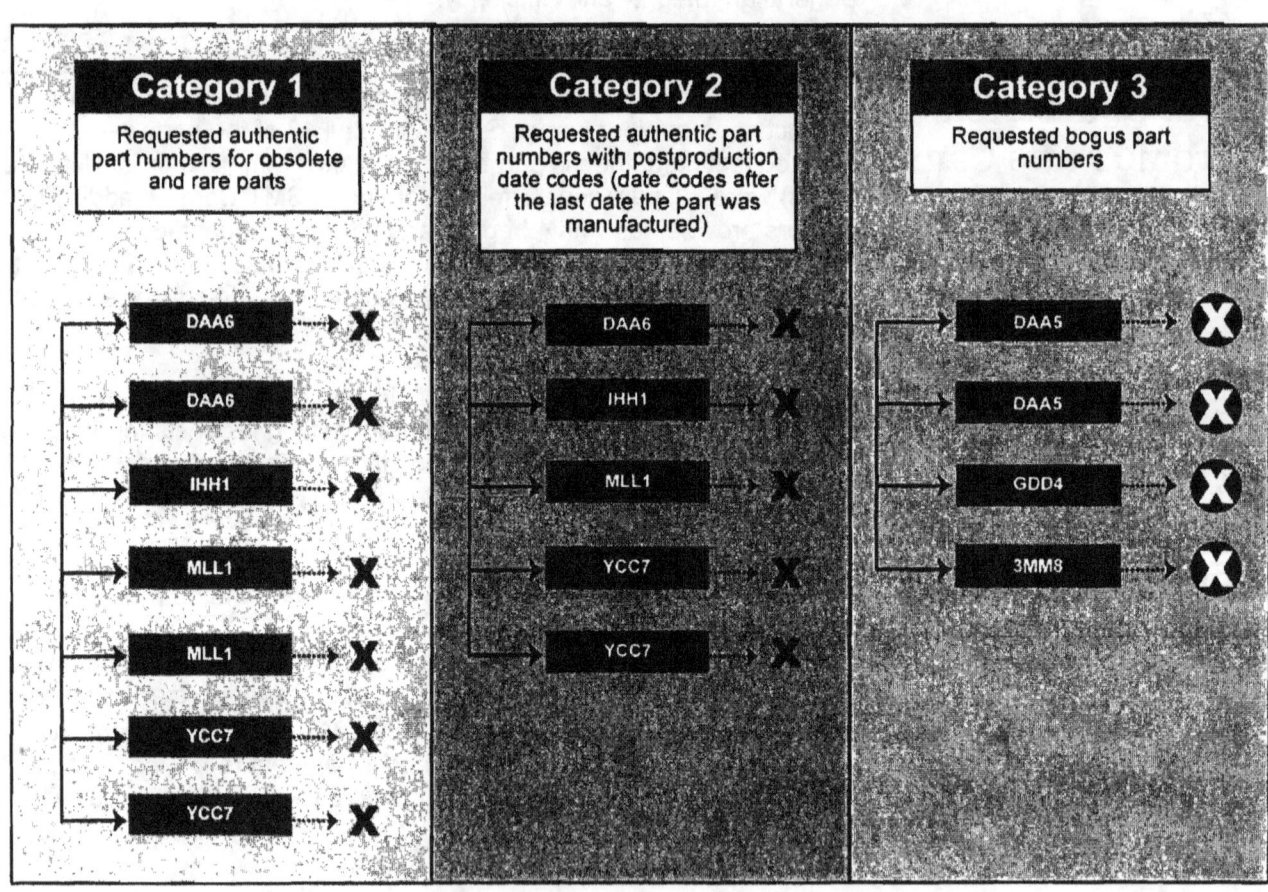

X - Suspect counterfeit part

Ⓧ - Bogus part

Source: GAO analysis of SMT test results.

Note: Part numbers shown have been altered from the part numbers used for purchasing.

GAO-12-375 Suspect Counterfeit Parts

Category 1: Authentic Part Numbers for Obsolete or Rare Parts

All seven of the obsolete or rare parts that SMT Corp. tested were suspected counterfeits. Each part failed multiple component authentication analyses, including visual, chemical, X-ray, and microscopic testing. The parts were purchased from five different vendors. Figure 2 provides photos and detailed test results for each part.

Category 1 Requested authentic part numbers for obsolete and rare parts							
Analysis performed	**DAA6**	**DAA6**	**IHH1**	**MLL1**	**MLL1**	**YCC7**	**YCC7**
Visual Inspection	Fail ☒	Fail ☒	Fail ☒	Fail ☒	Fail ☒	Fail ☒	Fail ☒
Resistance to Solvents (RTS) and Scrape Test	N/A	N/A	Fail ☒	N/A	N/A	Pass ✓	Pass ✓
Package Configuration and Dimensions	Pass ✓	Pass ✓	Pass ✓	Pass ✓	Pass ✓	Pass ✓	Fail ☒
X-Ray Florescence Elemental Analysis	Fail ☒	Fail ☒	Pass ✓	Fail ☒	Fail ☒	Pass ✓	Pass ✓
Real-Time X-ray Analysis	Pass ✓	Fail ☒	Pass ✓	Pass ✓	Pass ✓	Fail ☒	Pass ✓
Scanning Electron Microscopy (SEM) Analysis	Fail ☒	Fail ☒	Fail ☒	Pass ✓	Pass ✓	Fail ☒	Fail ☒
Solderability Test	Pass ✓	Pass ✓	Pass ✓	Pass ✓	Pass ✓	Pass ✓	Pass ✓
Dynasolve Test	N/A	N/A	Fail ☒	N/A	N/A	N/A	Fail ☒
Delidding and Die Microscopy	Fail ☒	Fail ☒	Fail ☒	Fail ☒	Fail ☒	Fail ☒	Pass ✓
Suspect counterfeit	**Yes**	**Yes**	**Yes**	**Yes**	**Yes**	**Yes**	**Yes**

Source: GAO analysis of SMT test results.

Note: Part numbers shown have been altered from the part numbers used for purchasing. N/A indicates that the analysis was not performed because the unique properties of the part render the test inapplicable or prevent the test from being performed.

DAA6 (two parts purchased). Both purchases made using part number DAA6 contained samples that failed multiple authentication analyses, leading SMT Corp. to conclude that the parts were suspect counterfeit.

Both parts were purchased from different vendors using the same part number, but were not identical, as shown in figure 2. An authentic part with this part number is an operational amplifier that may be commonly found in the Army and Air Force's Joint Surveillance and Target Attack Radar System; the Air Force's F-15 Eagle fighter plane; and the Air Force, Navy, and Marine Corps's Maverick AGM-65A missile. If authentic, this part converts input voltages into output voltages that can be hundreds to thousands of times larger. Failure can lead to unreliable operation of several components (e.g., integrated circuits) in the system and poses risks to the function of the system where the parts reside.

The part we received from one vendor failed four of seven authentication analyses. Visual inspection found inconsistencies, including different or missing markings and scratches, which suggested that samples were re-marked. Scanning electron microscopy (SEM) analysis revealed further evidence of re-marking. X-ray fluorescence (XRF) testing of the samples revealed that the leads contain no lead (Pb) instead of the 3 percent lead (Pb) required by military specifications.[8,9] Five samples were chosen for delidding, which exposes parts' die, because of their side marking inconsistencies. While all five samples had the same die, the die markings were inconsistent.[10] According to SMT Corp., die markings in components manufactured within the same date and lot code should be consistent. Finally, the devices found in the first lot tested went into "last time buy" status in 2001, meaning that the parts were misrepresented as newer than they actually were. The manufacturer confirmed this status and added that the part marking did not match its marking scheme, meaning that the date code marked on the samples would not be possible.

---

[8] XRF analyzers quickly and nondestructively determine the elemental composition of materials commonly found in microelectronic devices. Each of the elements present in a sample produces a unique set of characteristic x-rays that reveals the chemistry of the sample in a manner analogous to a fingerprint. A lead is an electrical connection consisting of a length of wire or soldering pad that comes from a device. Leads are used for physical support, to transfer power, to probe circuits, and to transmit information.

[9] DOD, *DOD Performance Specification for Integrated Circuits (Microcircuits) Manufacturing*, MIL-PRF-38535J (Dec. 28, 2010).

[10] A die is a small wafer of semiconducting material on which a functional circuit is fabricated.

The part received from the second vendor failed five of seven authentication analyses. Visual inspection again found inconsistencies, including additional markings on about half the samples. Further, scratches and reconditioned leads indicated that the parts were removed from a working environment—that is, not new as we requested. SEM analysis corroborated these findings. As with the other DAA6 part, XRF testing revealed that the leads contain no lead (Pb). X-rays revealed different sized die, and delidding revealed that the die were differently marked.

IHH1 (one part purchased). The purchase made using part number IHH1 contained samples that failed five of nine authentication analyses, leading SMT Corp. to conclude that the part was suspect counterfeit. An authentic part with this part number is a multiplexer, which allows electronic signals from several different sources to be checked at one location. It has been used in at least 63 different DOD weapon systems, including the Air Force Special Operations Forces' AC-130H Gunship aircraft, the Air Force's B-2B aircraft, and the Navy's E-2C Hawkeye aircraft. If at least one of the specific signals is critical to the successful operation of the system, then failure could pose a risk to the system overall.

Visual inspection revealed numerous issues, including color differences in the top and bottom of the part's surfaces, suggesting resurfacing and re-marking. Large amounts of scuffs and scratches, foreign debris, and substandard leads were also found. The part also failed resistance to solvents (RTS) testing when it resulted in removal of resurfacing material. Further, Dynasolve testing (additional RTS testing) revealed remnants of a completely different manufacturer and part number. SEM showed evidence of lapping, which is the precise removal of a part's material to produce the desired dimensions, finish, or shape. Finally, delidding showed die that were similar but insufficiently marked to determine whether they matched the authentic part number. However, because of the failure of the Dynasolve testing, the die cannot be correct.

MLL1 (two parts purchased). Both purchases made using part number MLL1 contained a number of samples that failed three of seven authentication analyses, leading SMT Corp. to conclude that the parts were suspect counterfeit. Both parts were purchased from different vendors using the same part number, but were not identical, as shown in figure 2. An authentic part with this number is a voltage regulator that may be commonly found in military systems such as the Air Force's KC-130 Hercules aircraft, the Navy's F/A-18E Super Hornet fighter plane, the

Marine Corps's V-22 Osprey aircraft, and the Navy's SSN-688 Los Angeles Class nuclear-powered attack submarine. If authentic, these parts provide accurate power voltage to segments of the system they serve. Failure can lead to unreliable operation of several components (e.g., integrated circuits) in the system and poses risks to the function of the system where the parts reside.

The parts received from both vendors failed the same authentication analyses. Visual inspection was performed on all evidence samples from both purchases. Different color epoxy seals were noted within both lots, according to SMT Corp., which is common in suspect counterfeit devices because many date and lot codes are re-marked to create a uniform appearance. Moreover, XRF testing of the samples revealed that the leads contain no lead (Pb); according to military performance standards, leads should be alloyed with at least 3 percent of lead (Pb).[11] Further, XRF data between the top and bottom of the lead revealed inconsistencies in chemical composition, leading SMT Corp. to conclude that the leads were extended with the intention to deceive. Microscopic inspection revealed that different revision numbers of the die and differences in various die markings were found even though the samples were advertised to be from the same lot and date code. Commonly, components manufactured within the same date and lot code will have the same die revisions. According to SMT Corp.'s report, the manufacturer also stated that "it is very unusual to have two die runs in a common assembly lot. This is suspicious." Finally, the devices found in the first lot tested went into "last time buy" status—an end-of-life designation—on September 4, 2001, meaning that the parts were misrepresented as newer than they actually were. The manufacturer confirmed this status and added that the part marking did not match its marking scheme, meaning that the date code marked on the samples would not be possible.

YCC7 (two parts purchased). Both purchases made using part number YCC7 contained samples that failed several authentication analyses, leading SMT Corp. to conclude that the parts were suspect counterfeit. Both parts were purchased from different vendors using the same part number. An authentic part with this part number is a memory chip that

---

[11] DOD, *DOD Performance Specification for Integrated Circuits (Microcircuits) Manufacturing.*

has been used in at least 41 different DOD weapons systems, including the ballistic missile early warning system, the Air Force's Peacekeeper missile and B-1B aircraft, the Navy's Trident submarine and Arleigh Burke class of guided missile destroyer, and the Marine Corps's Harrier aircraft. Failure of the chip, if not redundant, could pose risk to the overall system.

The part we received from one vendor failed four of seven authentication analyses. Visual inspection identified numerous issues, including bent or misshapen leads and lead ends and deformed, less-detailed logos of the claimed manufacturer. X-ray analysis revealed that various parts in the samples contained different sized die. SEM analysis showed that surface material had been precisely removed to allow for re-marking. Finally, delidding of two samples revealed die that were marked from a competitor manufacturer with a different part number than the one we requested. In addition, one die was marked with a 1986 copyright, while the other was labeled 1992.

The part received from the second vendor failed four of nine authentication analyses. Visual inspection showed evidence of re-marking, with the color of the top surfaces of samples not matching the color of the bottom surfaces. Some samples displayed faded markings while others were blank and had heavy scuff marks to suggest resurfacing. The markings were also not as clear and consistently placed as manufacturer-etched markings would be. Leads were substandard in quality, had been refurbished, and were not as thick as specified. Further, SEM showed evidence of lapping. Finally, the samples responded inconsistently to Dynasolve testing.

Category 2: Authentic Part Numbers with Postproduction Date Codes

Similarly, all five of the parts we received and tested after requesting legitimate part numbers but specifying postproduction date codes were also suspected counterfeit, according to SMT Corp. By fulfilling our requests, the four vendors that provided these parts represented them as several years newer than the date the parts were last manufactured, as verified by the part manufacturers. Figure 3 provides photos and detailed test results.

Category 2 Requested authentic part numbers with postproduction date codes (date codes after the last date the part was manufactured)					
Analysis performed	**DAA6**	**IHH1**	**MLL1**	**YCC7**	**YCC7**
Visual Inspection	Fail ☒	Fail ☒	Fail ☒	Fail ☒	Fail ☒
Resistance to Solvents (RTS) and Scrape Test	N/A	Fail ☒	N/A	Fail ☒	Fail ☒
Package Configuration and Dimensions	Pass ☑	Pass ☑	Pass ☑	Pass ☑	Pass ☑
X-Ray Florescence Elemental Analysis	Fail ☒	Pass ☑	Fail ☒	Pass ☑	Pass ☑
Real-Time X-ray Analysis	Pass ☑	Fail ☒	Pass ☑	Pass ☑	Pass ☑
Scanning Electron Microscopy (SEM) Analysis	Fail ☒	Fail ☒	Fail ☒	Fail ☒	Fail ☒
Solderability Test	Pass ☑	Fail ☒	Pass ☑	Pass ☑	Pass ☑
Dynasolve Test	N/A	Fail ☒	N/A	N/A	Pass ☑
Delidding and Die Microscopy	Fail ☒	Fail ☒	Fail ☒	Pass ☑	Pass ☑
Suspect counterfeit	**Yes**	**Yes**	**Yes**	**Yes**	**Yes**

Source: GAO analysis of SMT tst results.

Note: Part numbers shown have been altered from the part numbers used for purchasing. N/A indicates that the analysis was not performed because the unique properties of the part render the test inapplicable or prevent the test from being performed.

DAA6 (one part purchased). The purchase made using part number DAA6 contained samples that failed four of seven authentication analyses, leading SMT Corp. to conclude that the part was suspect counterfeit. Surfaces on the parts in the evidence lots were found to have scratches similar to suspect counterfeit devices that have been re-marked, as confirmed by both visual inspection and SEM analysis. In addition, the quality of exterior markings, including a lack of consistency between the manufacturer's logo, was lower than would be expected for authentic devices. Tooling marks were also found on the bottom of all components within the evidence lot; these marks suggest that the components were pulled from a working environment. Further inspection led SMT Corp. to conclude that many samples with refurbished leads were extended with the intention to deceive. Moreover, XRF analysis revealed the leads contain no lead (Pb) instead of the 3 percent lead (Pb) required by military specifications.[12] Delidding revealed that the die, while correct for this device, were inconsistent. As previously stated, multiple die runs are considered suspicious. Finally, some of the samples went into "last time buy" status in 2001, despite the fact that we requested parts from 2005 or later and the vendor agreed to provide parts from 2010 or later.

IHH1 (one part purchased). The purchase made using part number IHH1 contained samples that failed seven of nine authentication analyses, leading SMT Corp. to conclude that the part was suspect counterfeit. The part we received was supplied by a different vendor than the one that supplied the IHH1 part shown in figure 2. Visual inspection revealed numerous issues, including mismatching surface colors, many scratches and scuffs, foreign debris, and leads that were not uniformly aligned. SEM also showed evidence of lapping. RTS testing resulted in removal of resurfacing material, and surfaces faded when exposed to Dynasolve, which should not occur. Further, samples did not solder properly. Finally, X-rays indicated that different die were used within the samples. This was confirmed in delidding, which revealed inconsistencies in size, shape, and date markings. Of the two types of die found in the sample, one does not match the authentic part number.

MLL1 (one part purchased). The purchase made using part number MLL1 contained samples that failed four of seven authentication analyses, leading SMT Corp. to conclude that the part was suspect

---

[12] DOD, *DOD Performance Specification for Integrated Circuits (Microcircuits) Manufacturing.*

counterfeit. The part we received was supplied by a different vendor than the ones who supplied the MLL1 parts shown in figure 2. Visual inspection revealed scuffs and scratches indicative of re-marking, which was also seen in SEM analysis. Different colored epoxy seals and variegated sizes and colors of the center mounting slug were also seen. Leads also showed evidence of being refurbished with the intent to deceive. XRF testing of the samples revealed that the leads contain no lead (Pb); according to military performance standards, leads should be alloyed with at least 3 percent of lead (Pb).[13] Delidding revealed that die, though similar, had markings indicating different revisions, which is uncommon for die manufactured in the same date code. Finally, the devices went into "last time buy" status in 2001, whereas the tested parts showed a date code indicating they were made in 2008. The manufacturer confirmed this status.

YCC7 (two parts purchased). The two purchases made from different vendors using part number YCC7 contained samples that failed several authentication analyses, leading SMT Corp. to conclude that they were suspect counterfeit. The part we received from one vendor failed three of eight authentication analyses. Visual inspection identified numerous issues, including different colored surfaces that suggest re-marking and unknown residues that indicate improper handling or storage. SEM analysis showed that surface material had been precisely removed to allow for re-marking, similarly to a YCC7 part with legitimate date codes tested above. Further, according to the manufacturer, the legitimate version of this part was last shipped in 2003, whereas the tested part showed a manufacturing date code of 2006. RTS testing resulted in removal of the part marking.

The part received from the second vendor failed three of nine authentication analyses. Visual inspection detected numerous issues, including different colored surfaces that suggest re-marking. The markings were also substandard, lacking clarity and consistency in placement. RTS testing removed part markings, further suggesting re-marking. SEM showed evidence of lapping. Delidding revealed die that were consistent with the authentic part, but the date code showed evidence of re-marking to make them appear as if they had come from a

---

[13] DOD, *DOD Performance Specification for Integrated Circuits (Microcircuits) Manufacturing.*

homogenous lot. Finally, the manufacturer verified that it last shipped this part in 2003, whereas our samples were marked 2007, which according to SMT Corp., could not be possible.

Category 3: Bogus Part Numbers

We received offers from 40 vendors in China to supply parts using invalid part numbers, and we purchased four parts from four vendors to determine whether they would in fact supply bogus parts. (See fig. 4.) These were different vendors than the ones that supplied us with the suspect counterfeit parts. The invalid numbers were based on actual part numbers, but certain portions that define a part's performance specifications were changed. For example, one of our invalid numbers was for an actual voltage regulator but that operated at bogus specifications. None of the invalid part numbers were listed in DLA's Federal Logistics Information System and, according to selected manufacturers, none are associated with parts that have ever been manufactured. As such, we did not send the parts to SMT Corp. for authentication analysis.

Figure 4: Photos of Parts Received Despite Request for Invalid Part Numbers

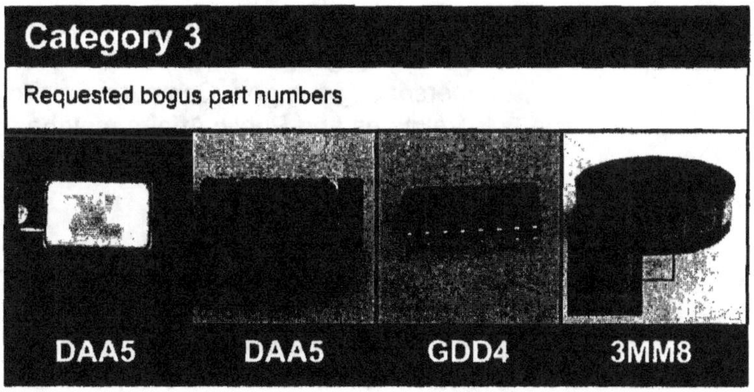

Source: GAO

Note: Part numbers shown have been altered from the part numbers used for purchasing.

We received the four bogus parts after requesting invalid part numbers DAA5, GDD4, and 3MM8. We made two orders using DAA5, one from each Internet purchasing platform, which were fulfilled by different vendors. The parts we received from each vendor appeared similar, as shown in figure 4. The similarity may be due to a number of factors. For example, the vendors could have simply ignored the invalid portion of the part numbers we requested (they did not contact us to inform us that the numbers were invalid). Another possible explanation could be that the parts happened to be fulfilled by the same vendor operating under two different names.

In furtherance of our investigation to determine the willingness of firms to provide us bogus parts, we created a totally fictitious part number that was not based on an actual part number and requested quotations over one Internet platform. We received an offer to supply the part from one vendor, but did not invest the resources to purchase the bogus part.

As agreed with your offices, unless you publicly announce the contents of this report earlier, we plan no further distribution until 30 days from the report date. At that time, we will send copies to the appropriate congressional committees, the Acting Under Secretary of Defense for Acquisition, Technology, and Logistics, and other interested parties. In addition, the report will be available at no charge on the GAO website at http://www.gao.gov.

If you or your staff have any questions about this report or need additional information, please contact Richard Hillman at (202) 512-6722 or hillmanr@gao.gov or Timothy Persons at (202) 512-6522 or personst@gao.gov. Contact points for our Offices of Congressional Relations and Public Affairs may be found on the last page of this report. Other key contributors to this report are listed in appendix II.

Richard J. Hillman
Managing Director
Forensic Audits and Investigative Service

Timothy Persons
Chief Scientist
U.S. Government Accountability Office

Appendix I: Details of Authentication Analysis Tests

This appendix provides details on each of the tests that constitute the authentication analysis SMT Corp. conducted for the parts we purchased.

Visual inspection: Visual inspection is performed on a predetermined number of samples (usually 100 percent) to look for legitimate nonconformance issues as well as any red flags commonly found within suspect counterfeit devices.

Resistance to solvents (RTS): A mixture of mineral spirits and isopropyl alcohol is used to determine the part marking resistance and pure acetone is used to remove any resurface material. This test is not performed on all parts. In some cases, resurfacing material would not be used by counterfeiters to re-mark a part; in others, the solvents would remove markings even on legitimate parts.

X-ray florescence (XRF) elemental analysis: The XRF gathers and measures the elements within a target area. This is used specifically for testing components for RoHS or Hi-Rel conformance, which refer to dangerous substances such as lead (Pb), cadmium (Cd), and mercury (Hg) that are commonly used in electronics manufacturing. For suspect counterfeit devices, it helps determine if a component has the correct plating for the specification it supposed to adhere to.

Package configuration and dimensions: This test measures key areas of the device to see if they fall within industry specifications.

Real-time X-ray analysis: X-ray analysis is performed on a predetermined number of samples (usually 100 percent). The internal construction of components is inspected (depending on the component package type) for legitimate issues such as broken/taut bond wires, electrostatic discharge damage, broken die, and so forth. For suspect counterfeit devices, the differences in die size/shape, lead frames, bond wire layout, and so forth are inspected.

Scanning electron microscopy: A scanning electron microscope is used to perform an exterior visual inspection—more in depth than the previous visual inspection. This is usually performed on a two-piece sample from the evidence lot. Depending on the package type, indications of suspect counterfeit devices are sought, including surface lapping, sandblasting, and sanding with regard to part marking removal.

Solderability: This test is usually for legitimate components to determine if they will solder properly when they are used in production.

Dynasolve: Dynasolve is a chemical used to break down epoxies in an effort to remove resurfacing material that is impervious to the standard RTS test.

Decapsulation/delidding and die verification: The die of a component is exposed with either corrosive materials or a cutting apparatus. This is done to inspect the die or "brain" of a component to determine its legitimacy. This process is performed on numerous samples to look for differences between samples, such as die metallization layout, revisions, part numbers, and so forth—all of which are red flags for suspect counterfeit parts.

Appendix II: GAO Contacts and Staff Acknowledgments

GAO Contacts	Richard J. Hillman, (202) 512-6722 or hillmanr@gao.gov Timothy Persons, (202) 512-6522 or personst@gao.gov
Staff Acknowledgments	Cindy Brown Barnes, Assistant Director; Gary Bianchi, Assistant Director; Virginia Chanley; Dennis Fauber; Barbara Lewis; Jeffery McDermott; Maria McMullen; Kimberly Perteet, Analyst in Charge; Ramon Rodriguez; and Timothy Walker made key contributions to this report.